OPEN to GOD

Deepening Your Devotional Life

JOYCE HUGGETT

**Including
28 Guided
Meditations**

INTERVARSITY PRESS
DOWNERS GROVE, ILLINOIS 60515

InterVarsity Press
P.O. Box 1400, Downers Grove, Illinois 60515

InterVarsity Press is the book-publishing division of InterVarsity Christian Fellowship, a student movement active on campus at hundreds of universities, colleges and schools of nursing in the United States of America, and a member movement of the International Fellowship of Evangelical Students. For information about local and regional activities, write Public Relations Dept., InterVarsity Christian Fellowship, 6400 Schroeder Rd., P.O. Box 7895, Madison, WI 53707-7895.

All Scripture quotations, unless otherwise indicated, are from the Holy Bible, New International Version. Copyright © 1973, 1978, International Bible Society. Used by permission of Zondervan Bible Publishers. Scripture quotations marked GNB are taken from the Good News Bible. Scripture quotations marked RSV are taken from the Holy Bible, Revised Standard Version. Scripture quotations marked JB are taken from the Jerusalem Bible.

Cover photograph: Michael Goss

ISBN 0-8308-1827-8

Printed in the United States of America ∞

Library of Congress Cataloging-in-Publication Data

Huggett, Joyce, 1937-
    Open to God/Joyce Huggett.
      p.   cm.
    Reprint. Originally published: London: Hodder & Stoughton, 1989.
    Includes bibliographical references.
    ISBN 0-8308-1827-8
    1. Devotional exercises. 2. Meditations. I. Title.
  BV4832.2.H744   1991
  248.3—dc20   *91-12040*
                                          CIP

15	14	13	12	11	10	9	8	7	6	5	4	3	2	1
03	02	01	00	99	98	97	96	95	94	93	92	91		

For
PAM
the soul-friend
who inspired me
to become
radically
open to God

Open to God: the Cassette

A music cassette has been produced as an optional accompaniment to this book, containing meditative songs and instrumentals which will assist preparation for prayer and can also be used in the meditations themselves. The following items from the cassette are mentioned in the text of the book:

The Lord's Prayer
The Magnificat
Spirit of the living God
Jesus, Lamb of God
Breathe on me
Lord, you gave me everything
To love only you
My peace
In silence my soul is waiting
Gabriel's oboe theme
Fisher of men
I gave my life for you
On Eagles' Wings
Adoration
Open to God
The Rose

Author's Note

For many years I have stored prayers and quotations in my prayer journal, and I sometimes fail to make a note of the place where I found them. My secretary and I made every effort to trace the source of the prayers and wise words I have quoted in this book, but in one or two instances our efforts proved abortive. If any reader knows the origin of these quotations, I would be glad to hear from them and will ensure that copyright is acknowledged in any reprint of *Open to God*.

Help Me to Say Yes . . .

Come and Worship . . .

Preface

This book is for those who ask nothing more of a book than that it contains the potential of drawing them closer to God.

One such person wrote to me after *The Joy of Listening to God* was published:

"In reading the book I felt a mixture of thrill and excitement and a sense of disappointment. A sense of excitement because of the possibilities which you have mapped out and the variety of different roads you suggest might be tried. But disappointment too because although I have a desire to walk closer to God and to listen to him, I know that desire isn't strong enough and persistent enough to keep me trying to break the barriers and blocks which inevitably occur.

"However, having read the book through rather rapidly, a proof of the excitement and enjoyment it gave is that I'm determined to go through it again more slowly and prayerfully."

I appreciated the mixture of anticipation and disillusionment expressed by this correspondent. Many who struggle to pray will identify with these feelings.

It is for such people that I have designed this new book. It contains hints to help those who, for a variety of reasons like busyness, disenchantment, distractions or ill health, have almost given up trying to be still before God. And it contains a series of meditations.

But the meditations are not for those who are looking for someone else to tell them what to think or feel. They are for those who are prepared to unearth for themselves the treasures which are buried in the Bible and hidden in their own hearts.

The reason for designing the meditations in this way is that individuals and groups who explore listening prayer often find that the nature of their times of quiet changes. As their hunger for God becomes more acute, the "fast food" approach of glancing first at a Bible passage and then at notes containing someone else's reflections on the passage leaves them undernourished and still ravenous. What they yearn for is a recipe which will show them how to mix a variety of prayer ingredients so that they can make for themselves a good, nourishing, homemade meal.

"So how am I supposed to spend my prayer time?" such people sometimes ask. "Do I spend it in adoration? Contemplate nature? Enter into the Gospels with all my senses? Or what?"

My response to such questions has been to produce some guidelines in the form of meditations. These meditations, like the introductory chapters of the book, are not so much reflections to read as work to be done. They have been written with the hope that the reader, having read through the chapter or the suggestions, will return to the text, experiment with the exercises and expect that insights will come which contain spiritual sustenance.

"New beginnings" was the theme in my mind as I began work on this project. And I dreamed a dream—that readers of all denominations who sense within themselves the call to love God with all their heart, with all their soul, with all their mind and with all their strength (Mt 22:37) would join me in using this material as another New Year dawns. That is why many of the meditations place the spotlight on the events which occurred within a few days and weeks of Jesus' birth.

But I am writing the book in the height of summer in Cyprus, not in winter, and I am discovering that the Annunciation, the birth and naming of Jesus, the visit of the Magi and the flight into Egypt speak just as powerfully when temperatures soar into the eighties as when snow powders the ground. And so three prayers have taken root inside me while I have been writing. The first is that readers will return to these pages often—sometimes to use the meditations consistently and sometimes just to "dip." The second is that through this book readers will discover that, with God, new beginnings are always possible. And the third is that the suggestions and meditations will indeed lead each reader deeper into God.

Acknowledgments

So many people have contributed to this book that writing it has been both a joy and a privilege. Alas! Here, there is space to mention by name only a handful of those who have given so generously of their time, their expertise and their encouragement.

My first vote of thanks goes to Sister Pamela CHN—the soul-friend with whom I love to lead retreats and weeks of guided prayer and to whom I have dedicated the book. Through her patient, caring listening and guidance while I was on retreat on one occasion, I discovered the life-changing discipline of opening myself to God in a new, prolonged and leisurely way.

I owe a similar debt of gratitude to Gerard Hughes. On another retreat, he listened to me with such skill and sensitivity that new vistas of meditation opened up for me—through which God drew me deeper and deeper into himself.

My third thank-you goes to Sister Theresa Margaret CHN whose path "happened" to cross mine just when I was looking for someone to illustrate this book. I thank God for allowing me to meet such a gifted person at that precise moment in time. When I first saw her prayerful interpretations of my text, I was deeply moved. They are meditations in themselves and continue to move me every time I contemplate them. While we have worked together on the book and on retreats, Sister Margaret has broadened my prayer horizons even further and I owe her an enormous debt of gratitude.

In addition to these three friends, I have been helped and encouraged by many people I have never yet met.

Sister Pauline Green of the Nodffa Retreat Centre readily agreed to allow me to use her own photographs of the potter at work and the clay. These are also obtainable on attractively produced cards.

Sister Catharine SLG graciously gave me permission to use the card which she designed and which has been very important to me for years. Her line drawing accompanies Meditation Six, and may be obtained from The Convent of the Incarnation.

And the German publisher Brendow Verlag was equally cooperative in sending me the negatives of Dorothea Steigerwald's *In Der Krippe* (Christchild in the Crib) and *In Deine Hand* (Child Resting on the Hand of God). Prayer cards are available from them.

The Return of the Prodigal hangs in West Malling Abbey, and I am grateful to the abbess for allowing my publisher to go there to photograph it. I am indebted to her also for granting permission to quote from some of the small prayer cards which come from the printing press at the Abbey. Each of these cards and pictures has played a significant part in my own pilgrimage of prayer and I am overjoyed now to be able to introduce them to a wider readership.

Among the others I must thank are my husband who, as always, supported and encouraged me while the book was taking shape and who took the picture of *The Light of the World* for me, and the Contemplative Prayer Group at my home church, St. Nicholas' Nottingham. Their fellowship on the prayer journey stimulates and supports me continually. I am also grateful to Pete and Maggie Bates for allowing me to reproduce a picture which hangs in their lounge—the batik representation of the person leaving the burden at the foot of the cross.

My thanks go to three more people: members of the editorial team at Hodder and Stoughton. David Wavre, Tim Anderson and Kathy Dyke have not only given me endless support and encouragement, they and others at Hodders have helped me to feel part of the Hodders family, for which I am really grateful.

Finally, I must mention my secretary. Rosalie Riem not only helped with the tedious, menial tasks which are part and parcel of writing a book, she also coped so skillfully and efficiently with my correspondence that I was set free to write. Rosalie, perhaps more than anyone, believed in this book as she watched it being born. I thank God for her quiet excitement as the book grew. Rosalie was killed in a car crash as the book was being printed, so I shall never have the joy of giving her a signed copy as I had planned. But I rejoice that her spirit lives on in these pages and that I can pay public tribute to her here.

CHAPTER 1

Completely Open

*L*ord, during these few days of stillness, may Joyce become radically open to you." That's a prayer a friend prayed for me just as I was going into retreat on one occasion.

Radically open. Those words seemed to puncture me and during those days of delicious withdrawal from the world, I echoed them frequently. I wanted truly to be open to God. Unequivocally, completely, entirely open.

Many others share this desire. I became acutely aware of this after my book *The Joy of Listening to God* was published. Many readers wrote to tell me that they, too, felt drawn to open up to God afresh.

But like the person I refer to in the preface, our attempts at openness do not always meet with unmitigated joy and success. Sometimes they result in seeming failure and joylessness. Our prayers scarcely seem to pierce the ceiling of the room in which we pray, let alone reach heaven itself. Our minds wander. And all sense of God's presence seems to evaporate.

Richard Foster reminds us that such disappointments are to be expected:

> When solitude is seriously pursued, there is usually a flush of initial success and then an inevitable letdown—and with it a desire to abandon the pursuit altogether. Feelings leave and there is a sense that we are not getting through to God.[1]

It is for those who have experienced such frustration but want to make a fresh start that I have designed this book. As I underlined in the preface, readers will glean most from these introductory chapters if, having read them straight through, they re-read one section at a time, pausing to ponder on the pictures, seeing the suggestions as work to be done and listening to the music, recognizing that music sometimes seeps into parts of our personality which words fail to reach and seems to bring us into the stillness which is a prerequisite for knowing God in the depths of our being.

A Recognition

Whenever we yearn to make a fresh start in our relationship with God, the place to begin is with the realization that the desire is, of itself, God's work. There is no need for us to struggle back to some spiritual starting line before we start to pray again. God chalks the starting line just where we are. Maria Boulding expresses this beautifully:

> All your love, your stretching out, your hope, your thirst, God is creating in you so that he may fill you. It is not your desire that

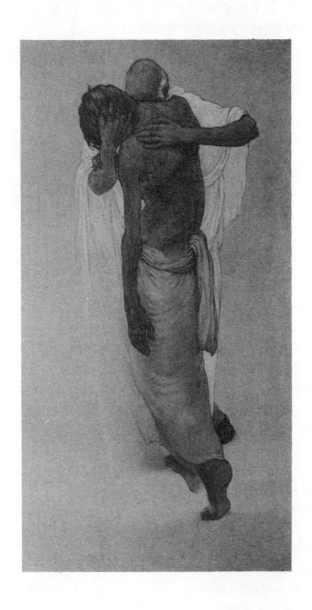

makes it happen, but his. He longs through your
heart. . . . In your prayer God is seeking you
and himself creating the prayer; he is on
the inside of the longing. . . . God's
longing for us is the spring of
ours for him."[2]

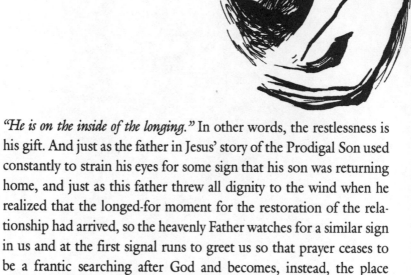

"He is on the inside of the longing." In other words, the restlessness is
his gift. And just as the father in Jesus' story of the Prodigal Son used
constantly to strain his eyes for some sign that his son was returning
home, and just as this father threw all dignity to the wind when he
realized that the longed-for moment for the restoration of the relationship had arrived, so the heavenly Father watches for a similar sign
in us and at the first signal runs to greet us so that prayer ceases to
be a frantic searching after God and becomes, instead, the place
where we are found, re-established and cherished by him.

Pause: *to drink in the truths that God loves us enough to wait and watch
and long for our return. And these:*
  Love says:
    before the worlds were made
    I chose you
    chose you to be mine
    in love and holiness
    and in my choosing

Love says:
before the worlds were made
I chose you
chose you to be mine
in love and holiness
and in my choosing
lies your choice of me
each for each
each in the other
all in the
One in Three

lies your choice of me
each for the other
each in the other
all in the
One in Three[3]

A Response

At the first signal from us God "runs to greet us."

Whenever I am tempted to fear that this claim might be extravagant or untrue, I turn to Holman Hunt's famous representation of Jesus' invitation: "Look, I am standing at the door, knocking. If one of you hears me . . . and opens . . . , I will come in to share his meal, side by side with him" (Rev 3:20 JB).

This invitation never fails to reassure me that no matter how lukewarm or inattentive or lacking in openness I may have become, God is still there—waiting. All I have to do is to open up to him and he will come to me with the warmth and closeness which is implied in that picture of two people sitting side by side over a special and intimate meal. And, as Basil Pennington points out, "we won't sit with a table between us. It will be side by side—like the beloved disciple who could lean over and rest his head upon his Master's bosom."[4]

God waits to indwell us and to fill us with yet more grace, more love, more wholeness and with his own fullness. But the God of the Bible never bulldozes his way into a person's life. He loves us enough to wait until, of our own free will, we invite him to come to us. In the language of Revelation 3:20, this means discovering that the handle of the door lies on the inside of our lives, not the outside, where the door can be forced open. It means opening this to God once more. Or, to return to the image of the wayward son, it means making a definite resolve to retrace our steps and come back to the Father even though we may return bedraggled, forlorn and flea-infested. Until we come face to face with the waiting Father,

we will never appreciate the degree of his warmth or his welcome.

A Prayer

When we open ourselves to God in this way, our prayer life changes. One person of prayer put it well: "Looking back," he said, "my impression is that for many, many years I was carrying prayer within my heart, but did not know it at the time. It was like a spring, but one covered by a stone. Then at a certain moment Jesus took the stone away. At that the spring began to flow and has been flowing ever since."[5]

The Holy Spirit's mission, among other things, is to create within the believer a similar spring of prayer. But if we are to enjoy this inflowing of divine life, we must ask for this gift of God's Spirit. This request can be made in a whole variety of ways. One is to request it using spontaneous prayers or well-tested ones: "Lord, teach us to pray" (Lk 11:1).

Or this prayer penned by George Appleton:

Lord,
I offer what I am
to what You are.
I stretch up to You in desire
my attention on You alone.
I cannot grasp You
*   explain You*
*   describe You*
Only cast myself into the depths
*   of your mystery*
Only let your love pierce the
*   cloud of my unknowing.*
Let me forget all but You
You are what I long for

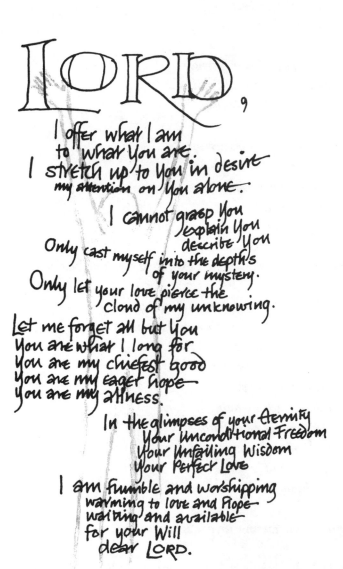

LORD,

I offer what I am
to what You are.
I stretch up to You in desire
my attention on You alone.

I cannot grasp You
explain You
describe You

Only cast myself into the depths
of your mystery.

Only let your love pierce the
cloud of my unknowing.

Let me forget all but You
You are what I long for
You are my chiefest good
You are my eager hope
You are my allness.

In the glimpses of your eternity
Your Unconditional Freedom
Your Unfailing Wisdom
Your Perfect Love

I am frumble and worshipping
warming to love and hope
waiting and available
for your Will
dear LORD.

You are my chiefest good
You are my eager hope
You are my allness.

In the glimpses of your Eternity
   Your Unconditional Freedom
   Your Unfailing Wisdom
   Your Perfect Love
I am humble and worshipping
   warming to love and hope
   waiting and available
   for your Will
     dear Lord.[6]

Or Dean Eric Milner-White's expressed desire to be open to God:

Speak, Lord, for your servant is listening.
   0 Lord, my heart is ready, my heart is ready;
   my mind awake, attent, alert;
   my spirit open and ardent,
   abandoning all else,
   holding itself in leash,
   straining the eye of faith,
   hearkening for your step, distant and nearer,
   leaping with love,
   throbbing loudly, yet lying still;

Speak, Lord, for your servant is listening.[7]

Pause: *Look carefully at* The Return of the Prodigal. *Pray one of the prayers above or listen to* Breathe on me *or* Spirit of the Living God *on the tape.*

Speak, Lord, for your servant is listening.
O Lord, my heart is ready, my heart is ready;
My mind awake, attent, alert;

my spirit open and ardent,
abandoning all else

Holding itself in leash,
straining the eye of faith,

hearkening for your step, distant and nearer,

leaping with love,

throbbing loudly, yet lying still;

'Speak, Lord, for your servant is listening.'

A Prayer Place

When we have recognized that God is wooing us back to himself and when we have made our response to this call of love, our next need is to find a place where we can relax with him. Jesus emphasizes the importance of such a place: " 'When you pray, go into your room, close the door and pray to your Father, who is unseen' " (Mt 6:6).

Jesus had no room into which he could retreat. Instead, he withdrew frequently to certain lonely places so that he could relate to his Father without hindrance or disturbance. If Jesus needed a "lonely place," how much more do we need a refuge where we will not be disturbed by the telephone or the doorbell; a place, if possible, which is not battered by the sounds and vibrations of frenetic energies.

As Basil Pennington explains, such activities and loud, hard music carry their charge long after they have ceased. They take their toll on us and drain us of the vital energy we need if we are to be radically open to God.[8]

Some of us are fortunate. We have a choice of places and can therefore take these observations into consideration. We can turn a spare bedroom or a garden shed into a prayer room. Others have to be more creative. A friend of mine uses a certain chair in her living room as her prayer place. Another goes to a certain corner of her bedroom to pray. I have converted a portion of our loft into a delightful chapel where I can shut out all interruptions and where I can "just be" with Jesus.

Others are less fortunate and more creative. I think, for example, of a woman I once met whose husband hated to see her praying. When I asked her how she coped with this crisis she told me that every evening she and her husband watched television together. During the commercials she would close her eyes. Her husband thought she was snoozing but she was spending a few quiet moments with

God. And, of course, despite the noise and the distractions, God honored these few snatched moments with him.

This woman reinforced Brother Ramon's observation that, just as people in love "always manage to find a place to be alone together, to be lost in each other's presence, and to enter into loving and intimate communion,"[9] so people who are serious about deepening their relationship with God create a place where they can meet with him. When they find such a place they may well discover that, over a period of time, a powerful atmosphere is generated so that their sanctuary becomes prayer-saturated. Still. A corner of the world where God's presence is uniquely felt.

Pause: *Do you have a prayer place? If not, think creatively until you find a suitable spot. Start by asking yourself if there is anywhere nearby—a church maybe or a particular walk or beauty spot where the sense of God's presence is strong. Or maybe there is a corner of your home which could be converted into a "prayer place"—a certain chair or beanbag; a rug or particular spot on a certain carpet; a spare bedroom or closet; a garden shed.*

If you already have a prayer place, make some small alteration to it which expresses your renewed desire to be open to God. You could put a candle there which you light whenever you come to pray. Or you could buy a new poster or make a banner or put a cross there. Expect one day to experience in your prayer place what Jacob experienced at Bethel: "Truly, Yahweh is in this place and I never knew it! . . . How awe-inspiring this place is! This is nothing less than a house of God; this is the gate of heaven!" (Gen 28:16-17 JB).

Play the song In silence my soul is waiting *from the tape.*

Create a Space

A prayer place is of little use unless we carve out a space where we can step off the treadmill and give time to developing our relationship with God. Most people do not find this easy. We all complain

that time to pray is hard to come by. Yet we make time for the people
we really want to meet and the activities which really matter to us.
We do have time, as Michel Quoist rightly reminds us—all the time
that God gives:

> *The years of my life,*
> *The days of my years,*
> *The hours of my days,*
> *They are all mine.*
> *Mine to fill, quietly, calmly,*
> *But to fill completely, up to the brim* . . .[10]

The challenge which faces each of us is to discover the best possible
time when we can be alone with God. For many people, this will be
early morning. For others the deep-down stillness of the night will
provide them with the ideal setting for prayer.

When we pray matters little. What matters more is that we pray—
and that, wherever possible, we establish a rhythm of prayer—like
a certain peasant whose perseverance inspired his parish priest. Such
was this man's love for God that on his way to and from work each
day, he would pause outside his village church, deposit his spade,
his hoe and his pickaxe and slip into the building where he would
simply sit and soak up God's love.

One day his priest asked him, "My good father, what do you say
to our Lord in those long visits you pay him every day and many
times a day?"

"I say nothing to Him," the peasant replied. "I look at Him, and
He looks at me. And we tell each other that we love each other."[11]

We, too, need the opportunity to turn the eyes and ears of our
soul God-wards, to fix them there, to hear God speak words of
supportive love and to have an opportunity to respond.

Some of us will have the luxury of a whole hour a day in which
we can do this. Many will not. We must therefore learn to be real-
istic, to learn to pray as we can and not to strive to pray as we can't;

to learn to adapt our rhythm of prayer to the rhythm of our life.

What I mean by this is that the mother who faces the challenge of clamoring children morning, noon and night will almost certainly have to content herself with snatched minutes for prayer rather than leisurely hours—except on weekends when her husband might be persuaded to look after the children for a while so that his wife can rest in God. Or shift-workers: nurses, doctors on call, laborers, will find it impossible to be quiet at the same time every day. Their prayer pattern will have to be adjusted to the timetable which is set out for them by their employers.

God understands this and, far from being the hard taskmaster some of us make him out to be, he is gentle and generous. He is less concerned about when we come than that we *do* come. He longs for us to come because he loves to be with us and because he knows that it is in our best interest to meet with him. In his presence we receive fullness of joy, strength for the day, hope and a sense of direction for the future.

Pause: *to ask yourself whether you are a "nightingale" or an "owl"— more alert in the morning or the evening. Decide when you will carve out time for stillness and roughly how long this will normally be: five minutes, ten minutes, twenty minutes, an hour. Could you spend more time in prayer on the weekend? When? Earmark this time in your diary so that nothing else is allowed to crowd it out.*

Creating "Kingdom Moments"

One way of coming to God is to take advantage of life's "little solitudes," to borrow Richard Foster's phrase—those early-morning moments in bed before the family wakes up, that cup of coffee in the middle of the morning, sitting in bumper-to-bumper traffic during the rush hour, traveling by train or by car, standing in line in the supermarket. Snippets of time I once heard dubbed "Kingdom

moments." We can train ourselves to sense the presence of the in-
dwelling Christ in such moments just as Mary did when God's Son
was forming in her womb:

She who began by enclosing God within her womb, herself needs
no enclosure. . . . Hers the busy day of cooking, washing, sweep-
ing, shopping at the noisy bazaar, sewing, mending, nursing, but
through it all, the awe-inspiring love-union with the Lord.[12]

Commuters and journalists, politicians and film producers, pilots
and firemen, office workers and social workers and others whose
workday is notoriously stressful might envy Mary and question
whether there are many "Kingdom moments" in their day.

There are. The challenge comes to each of us to recognize them,
as George Sinker emphasizes in his book *Jesus Loved Martha*. He
encourages his readers, for example, to remind themselves of two
verses of Scripture when they wake up: "Get up and pray" (Lk

22:46) and "Very early in the morning, while it was still dark, Jesus got up, left the house and went off to a solitary place, where he prayed" (Mk 1:35).

It is Jesus who comes and wakes you, by whatever means He uses, and invites you to spend the first moments of the day with Him. Why? From His point of view, because He loves you and desires your company. From your point of view, because He knows it will be another tiring day and He wants to pour into you the strength and courage, the patience and peace to face each test the day will bring.[13]

Or again, he suggests that when we use the bathroom we turn our mind to Jesus and the man at the Pool of Siloam (Jn 9:7). "Go, wash," Jesus said to this man. And he adds:

Jesus bids us wash. But washing to Him always signified the sacrament of a clean heart. Washing in the Bible is a double action, bodily and spiritual. If we were to form that habit of thought, we would come consciously into His presence every time we washed, receiving the cleansing of His forgiveness and reunion with Him.[14]

And we would use the prayer of the psalmist: "Wash me, and I will be whiter than snow" (Ps 51:7).

Dressing is another activity which can so easily be combined with prayer. Recall Romans 13:14, suggests George Sinker: "Clothe yourselves with the Lord Jesus Christ." To be clothed with Christ means to be clothed with "His beauty, His strength, His love, His understanding, His patience, His peace, His joy. There is no end to the glory of this garment which He offers you to put on first thing every day."[15]

Even dishwashing can remind us of Jesus' promises and presence if we recall Jesus' command "Clean the inside of the cup and dish" (Mt 23:26). As we wash the dishes or load the dishwasher we can pray the psalmist's prayer: "Create in me a pure heart, O God, and renew a steadfast spirit within me" (Ps 51:10). This way, just as St. Teresa found God so easily among the pots and pans and just as Brother Lawrence learned how to cast the occasional loving gaze at God when elbow-deep in potato peelings, so we will find that even a kitchen can become a haven if we tune in to the sound of God's silence no matter what is going on around us.

Pause: *Make a list of possible "Kingdom moments" that you and God could enjoy together—over the ironing, the bed-making, traveling to and from work. Apply the principles I have sketched in this section. Use these "little solitudes" to the full. In addition, begin every meal time with a prayer—sometimes in silence. Ask that your eyes may be opened so that you can see Jesus. (See Lk 24:30-31.) Recognize the value of establishing a regular rhythm of prayer.*

Use regularly a prayer like this one which was written by Jane Austen:
Give me grace, almighty Father,
To address you with my heart,
—as well as my lips.
You are everywhere present,
From you no secret can be hidden.
Teach me to fix my thoughts on you
Reverently and with love,
So my prayers are not in vain.[16]

Tune In to the Sounds of Silence

But tuning in to silence is rarely easy in our modern world. Richard Foster explains why: "In contemporary society our Adversary majors in three things: noise, hurry, and crowds. If he can keep us engaged in 'muchness' and 'manyness,' he will rest satisfied."[17]

He will remain satisfied because "muchness" and "manyness" siphon off emotional energy, distort our perception and lead to exhaustion. And tired people find it almost impossible to relax sufficiently to open their innermost selves to God.

Is that why God pleads with us to "be still" (Ps 46:10)? Is that why he woos us into the wilderness where his voice can more easily be heard (Hos 2:14)? Probably. And it is why the next chapter of this book concentrates on the question: How can we best go down into the re-creating stillness of God?

Pause: *to pray:*
Drop thy still dews of quietness,
Till all our strivings cease:
Take from our souls the strain and stress,
And let our ordered lives confess
The beauty of thy peace.[18]

CHAPTER 2

Opening Up

*J*ust as the petals of a water lily uncurl when the sun shines, so closed parts of people unfold when they are silent. This is why both a still place and a regular appointment with God are so important to the person of prayer.

Silence is vital for a number of reasons. Silence is the context in which God most readily reveals himself, in which his voice is most clearly heard and where he rains on us the riches of his love. Silence is the language of lovers. It is therefore the language God delights to use to woo us to himself and the vocabulary we choose to express our response to his love. Silence before God has little to do with achieving but a great deal to do with receiving. In silence, we gather energy, receive guidance, gain God's perspective, discern his priorities and find refreshment. It is essential for the person of prayer to learn how to drop into this re-creative stillness which is so manifestly enriching:

> If we are to witness to Christ in today's marketplaces, where there are constant demands on our whole person, we need silence. If we are to be always available, not only physically, but by empathy, sympathy, friendship, understanding and boundless *caritas,* we need silence. To be able to give joyous, unflagging hospitality, not only of house and food, but of mind, heart, body and soul, we need silence.[1]

But silence is important for another reason. In silence we come face to face with ourselves. So often, while claiming, believing and singing that "Jesus is Lord," our lives center not around him but around "number one." Self. When we are still, this inconsistency is highlighted, and we become aware of our need to de-throne self and enthrone Christ afresh.

Tune the Instrument at the Gate

One way of ensuring that our times with God become less frenzied and more still is, to use the language of John Donne, to "tune the instrument at the gate"; to unwind as much as possible before we ever enter our place of prayer and to turn our thoughts and affection toward God before we utter a single word to him. In other words, it means prefixing our times of quiet with a period of pre-prayer.

Some people find that this prelude to prayer happens naturally: while they wash, while they tidy the house or their desk or while they do dishes they begin to anticipate the moment when they will cross the threshold of their prayer place to spend time alone with God. This way they tune in to God's wavelength and come to prayer eager and ready for a fresh encounter with Christ.

Pray in Tongues

Another way of dropping into the grand silence of God is to pray
in tongues—a beautiful, God-given but mysterious language which
bypasses the intellect and sometimes brings in its wake an intense
awareness of God's presence and power.

Music

Yet another way to still our whirring minds is to listen to meditative
music. Music soothes weary brains and bodies. It melts hard hearts.
And it reaches depths in a person into which words cannot trickle.
That is why we have produced a tape for readers to use alongside
this book.

There are other well-tried ways of relaxing in God's presence. This
exercise is a favorite one:

Tighten all your muscles and clench your fists until your whole
body is screwed up and tense. Then, starting from the top of your
head and working downwards, gradually relax one muscle at a
time—facial muscles, neck muscles, shoulders, arms, unclench
your fists and so on right down to your big toe.

And Brother Ramon has popularized this one:

Take off your shoes and wear a track suit or other loose clothing.
Everything free, everything easy, no strain. Now lie down upon
the ground on your back, and very simply enumerate the parts
and areas of your body, from your feet . . . calves . . . thighs . . .
buttocks . . . abdomen . . . arms . . . hands . . . shoulders . . . neck
. . . to your face and head. As you enumerate, stretch and gently
relax each part . . . letting go . . . letting go . . . until you have
drained the tension away and you are at rest. Resting naturally,
and resting in God.[2]

Listen to the Taize chant *My peace* and let it lead you into silence.

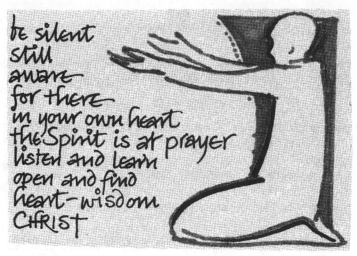

Pause: *Try some of these exercises for yourself. See which ones work for you. Use the ones you find helpful. Forget about the others for the time being. But come back to them on a subsequent occasion when you are finding stillness difficult again. Meditate on these words:*

> be silent
> still
> aware
> for there
> in your own heart
> the Spirit is at prayer
> listen and learn
> open and find
> heart-wisdom
> > Christ[3]

Alertness and Attentiveness

We rest our body in this way so that inwardly we might become alert, attentive, aware, available and receptive to every breath of God's Spirit. For prayer is like keeping an appointment with the

Living God who longs to reveal himself. All our antennae must therefore be alerted so that we pick up each and every signal he sends.

The kind of alertness I am describing is not unlike the round-the-clock attentiveness a mother gives to her newborn baby. There are leisurely periods each day when she gives her child her full attention, feeding him, bathing him and playing with him. And there are other times when she busies herself with her chores, her husband or her friends. Her child may lie in his pram in the garden while she works in the kitchen. Even so, she will sense when her infant needs her. Even when she is asleep, she will remain semi-attentive to his mood.

Similarly, we can enjoy fleeting reminders of God's love at odd moments during the day and we can also relax with him in our times of leisurely prayer.

There are a whole variety of ways of ensuring that all our senses are awake and ready for an encounter with God. One way is simply to gaze at a picture like the one on page 36 and to be present in it. We imagine ourselves kneeling at the foot of the cross alongside John and Mary, and we allow the love of Jesus expressed there to flow into us until we become increasingly open and attentive to the divine love and voice and until this love draws from us a heart response.

Another way is to imagine that we are entering a spacious building. The door swings open to let us in, and we walk down long and imposing corridors until we reach an open door. On the other side of the door we notice a figure of someone who is already coming to greet us. This person is Jesus. We register the way he greets us. We become aware, too, of the way we feel about that greeting and the nature of the response we find ourselves wanting to make.

Yet another way, if the grandeur of the building in the above exercise makes us uncomfortable, is to imagine that we are a rabbit playing in a field. Suddenly, some signal reminds us that it is time to encounter our Creator face to face. We kick up our back legs and scurry into our warren where we find Jesus waiting for us—deep down inside of the burrow of our existence.

These pictures symbolize the fact that we are indwelt by God. That is not to say that his presence in us can be localized in any way, but it does mean that with our imagination we can come close to Christ at the core of our being and appreciate the reason why prayer, of necessity, is a journey inwards.

Pause: *Go to your place of prayer and practice some of these "ways in" to stillness for yourself. If one, in particular, helps you to drop into stillness and become more aware of the felt presence of Jesus, make a habit of using it and forget about the others.*

Or you might like to experiment with this suggestion of Richard Foster's:

"Palms Down, Palms Up"

Begin by placing your palms down as a symbolic indication of your desire to turn over any concerns you may have to God. Inwardly you may pray, "Lord, I give to You my anger toward John. I release my fear of my dentist appointment this morning. I surrender my anxiety over not having enough money to pay the bills this month. I release my frustration over trying to find a baby-sitter for tonight." Whatever it is that weighs on your mind or is a concern to you, just say, "palms down." Release it. You may even feel a certain sense of release in your hands.

After several moments of surrender, turn your palms up as a symbol of your desire to receive from the Lord. Perhaps you will pray silently: "Lord, I would like to receive Your divine Love for John, Your peace about the dentist appointment, Your patience, Your joy." Whatever you need, you say, "palms up."

Having centered down, spend the remaining moments in complete silence. Do not ask for anything. Allow the Lord to commune with your spirit, to love you. If impressions or directions come, fine; if not, fine.[4]

The Body at Prayer

One of the quickest ways of stilling ourselves in the presence of God is to enlist the help of the body. The body can welcome God. Indeed, almost literally, our bodies can open up to God.

Open hands illustrate this. If, in our place of prayer, we stand or kneel and open our hands, we may find that they are "speaking"— saying: "Here I am, Lord—radically open to you." By moving our hands ever so slightly we communicate other non-verbal messages. By cupping our hands, for example, we might be saying: "I am ready to receive whatever you choose to give me." Or by cradling our hands in our laps we can beckon God and ask him to come. Or again if we stretch out our hands to God, we greet and welcome him.

Similarly, we can enlist other parts of our body as partners in prayer. A favorite prayer posture of mine is the prostrate position when I lie on the floor face downwards with my head resting on my hands, a cushion or the carpet if it is soft enough. Sometimes this seems to be the only adequate language in my vocabulary to express my littleness and God's greatness; my emptiness and God's fullness; my sinfulness and God's holiness; my poverty and God's abundance; my weakness and God's great strength; and my desire to become one with this overflowing God.

Openness to God can also be expressed by lying on one's back. This is arguably the most open bodily posture we can adopt, because it is a position which leaves us totally exposed to the living God. Nothing hidden.

Come let us kneel before the Lord our maker Ps 95.6

Our knees are also allies. Kneeling expresses humility, an appropriate sense of unworthiness, gratitude that the King of kings invites us into his presence. For those who like to spend much of their prayer time on their knees, a prayer stool is an invaluable aid. With it, a person can kneel for a long period of time without cutting off the circulation from their legs.

Standing also expresses reverence, alertness, adoration and submission: "Lord, I *am* ready—not simply to hear you and see you but to receive you and obey you also." Standing in prayer, though out of vogue, it seems, among Christians in the West, was a posture frequently adopted in Bible times.

While one is standing or kneeling, the arms can also "speak." As one of Job's friends put it: "If you set your heart aright, you will stretch out your hands toward him" (Job 11:13 RSV). Or as the psalmist experienced: "Every day I call upon thee, O LORD; I spread out my hands to thee" (Ps 88:9 RSV). Some people find that raised arms speak of joy, thanksgiving and praise while arms dropped by the thighs and upraised palms speak of self-surrender and submission. Folded arms also speak a language of their own. For some they signify a sense of unworthiness, for others, penitence, and for others, self-surrender.

Many pray-ers prefer to sit while they pray. This is partly because it is the most restful position and, without the distraction of physical discomfort of any kind, full attention can be given to the prayer as it unfolds. Such people usually find that the best kind of chair to use is one with a firm back but which is low enough to make it possible for both feet to rest flat on the floor in comfort.

With their back straight, their head upright and their hands "speaking" in whatever way seems appropriate, their whole body becomes alert to an awareness of the presence of God.

Each person is unique and each will therefore find their own favorite bodily posture to express a whole variety of messages. There is no right or wrong way to sit or kneel or stand or stretch out. Whatever helps is the position to be adopted. Victor Poucel puts the situation well:

Let us return to the proper use of our bodies. . . . Left to itself, it only knows how to sleep or to torment you. Clumsy and unclaimed, it has, in its naivety, taught you many things. But you never realized that you could avoid being kicked by Brother Ass by mounting him. He is ready to respond if only he can feel you in the saddle! Yes, our bodies pray.[5]

Pause: *Go to your prayer place. Experiment with the various bodily postures and hand gestures I have described. Find the ones which are most expressive for you and over the next few weeks use them regularly until they become a part of you and you stop feeling silly when you use them. Or try some traditional ones for yourself:*

☐ *beating the breast to signify repentance*

☐ *making the sign of the cross as you ask God to be especially present*

☐ *while kneeling, stretch out your hands and arms as a sign of self-surrender*

☐ *stand in God's presence with your head bowed to express reverence*

☐ *or make up gestures of your own*

Take one of the prayers from this book, or the Lord's Prayer, and find "body language" to express what the words are struggling to say. And play some of the music on the tape, like Adoration *or* Open to God *or* The Rose, *and respond to it by moving your hands, your arms or maybe your whole body in whatever way seems most appropriate to you.*

Breathing

Just as our bodies can either help or hinder our ability to be still before God, so our breathing can be an aid or an obstacle as we seek to be silent. Morton Kelsey encourages us to recognize its relationship to openness:

Learning how to use our lungs is one way of opening our spirits

to new life and stilling the turmoil of our minds and emotions.
... The effect of controlled breathing is almost like communication with the less conscious parts of one's being saying to them:
Simmer down and listen; there is something beyond this turmoil.[6]
If our breathing is to bring us quickly into silence, we need first to
concentrate on it without trying to change its rhythm in any way. As
we focus on the cool air entering the nostrils and the warm air leaving
our body, our breathing will automatically become deeper and slower
and a stillness will probably begin to creep over us. When this
happens, it can be helpful to think of the in-breathing as a symbol of
the breath and life of God's Spirit and the out-breathing as a symbol
of our surrender of ourselves (with our worries and pressures) to God.

Most people are surprised, the first time they try this, to discover
what a difference this simple exercise makes. The mind is free and
empty, sensing a greater clarity and repose, ready to rest in the
Lord. The rhythm of our whole body, and not just of our breathing, has slowed down, quieted, and is supportive of our finding
the deep quiet within.[7]

The advantage of this "way in" to stillness is that it can be practiced
unobtrusively in an airport, a train or on a bus journey, and it brings
us very quickly to the threshold of God's presence.

One way of ensuring that the stillness becomes Jesus-centered is
to re-focus from the hectic schedule which dominates our life onto
Jesus himself. And one of the most effective ways of doing that is
to whisper his name while we are deepening our breathing. While
you inhale, say the first part of the name, _Je-,_ and as you exhale, say
the second part, _-sus._ I sometimes like to think of this as a way of
calling out to God in the way I might call out a welcome or a
greeting to my husband. At other times, as I breathe in, I envisage
God's Spirit coming to me afresh—and as I breathe out saying
_"-us,"_ I pray Paul's mental prayer that it may be no longer I who live
but Christ who lives in me. The "us" represents the "me."

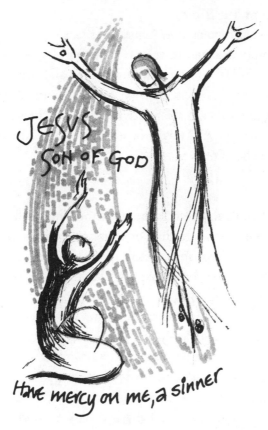

"*Je-sus.*" This prayer is a shortened version of *The Jesus Prayer.* Some people find it more helpful to pray the complete prayer as they "center down": "Lord Jesus Christ, Son of God, have mercy on me a sinner."

Pause: *Practice the breathing exercise I have outlined and whisper the name of Jesus or some other phrase or sentence. Practice this regularly for a few weeks. If it helps you, take it on board as you pray. If you find it intrusive or cumbersome, lay it aside. Remember always to "pray as you can, not as you can't."*

Listen to the prayer on the tape: Jesus, Lamb of God.

Meditation on the Bible

One method of dropping into stillness was handed down to us from the fifth century or even earlier. It is commonly known as *Lectio Divina*, a term which signifies a prayerful reading and pondering of the Scriptures which "has contemplation as its assumed culmination."[8] Since Latin is no longer a familiar language for most of us, "the practice of the four R's" might be a better way of describing this powerful method of prayer.

Read

The first R stands for Read because this praying of the Scriptures begins with a meditative reading of a passage from the Bible. In the earliest days of Christianity, Jesus' disciples were not fortunate enough to own a Bible for themselves. They therefore listened to the Scriptures being read to them. As they did so, they waited until a phrase or word or sentence attracted them.

Our aim as we read slowly and deliberately and meditatively is similar—to listen to the words and to wait until a short phrase or sentence or a single word draws us to itself or appeals to us in some mysterious way. If this is to happen, instead of reading a passage just once or skim reading, it is usually necessary to read the passage several times giving it our full attention until we are truly attuned to it; to move from the first R to the second.

Receive

Our goal is to personalize the words; to receive them as though God had written them for us at this precise moment in time. Indeed, the aim of this attentive reading is to spend time alone with God, to discover more about him and to hear what he wants to say to us. I sometimes liken this reading to finding a fallen leaf in autumn or catching a snowflake in winter. Just as children and some adults take delight in turning over and over in their hands such pieces of God's creation, contemplating them, so the person of prayer can hold a piece of Scripture in mind and heart—focus, dwell, stand guard over, ponder and brood on it and prepare to penetrate it with the intention of receiving and savoring it so that through it the person encounters God personally.

Recite: Or again, I sometimes liken it to reading a letter from someone we love. It frequently happens that, as we read, a small phrase will trigger an unexpected reaction or awaken our curiosity. Even when we have put the letter away, we discover that those few words have lodged in our minds and captured our imagination. They tumble around our brain exciting us or troubling us. We find ourselves repeating them over and over.

And that is precisely what these early Christians did with "their" phrase. They would recite it and commit to memory the words which had attracted them. As we recite, memorize and welcome the Word which has awakened in us a response and as we ponder it, we are receiving it in such a way that, eventually, we may hear far more from God than these few words seem at first to convey.

Regurgitate: And we find that, slowly and gradually, as we give our assent to God's Word, we are being changed by it—mysteriously and imperceptibly. Basil Pennington suggests that this transforming process is not unlike cows chewing the cud:

> A cow goes out and fills its stomach with grass or other food. Then it settles down quietly and through the process of regurgitation reworks what it has received, moving its lips in the process. Thus it is able fully to assimilate what it has previously consumed and to transform it into rich, creamy milk.

He likens the creamy milk to love empowered by the Holy Spirit, adding: "When the received word passes from the lips into the mind and then down into the heart through constant repetition, it produces in the one praying a loving, faith-filled response."[9]

Another picture which helps me to understand what is happening through this process comes from the pen of Gerard Hughes in his outstanding book *God of Surprises:*

> The process is analogous to sucking a boiled sweet. Do not try to analyse the phrase just as you would not normally break up a boiled sweet and subject it to chemical analysis before tasting. Often a phrase will catch the attention of our subconscious mind's needs long before our conscious mind is aware of the reason for the attraction.[10]

I like that. But because boiled sweets spoil our teeth, I prefer to liken the process to the slow sucking of a strong throat lozenge. We select our Bible lozenge, suck it as slowly as possible, savor it, and feel its healing properties oozing into the innermost recesses of our being, trusting that the Holy Spirit knows precisely those parts of us which need to be soothed or touched, challenged or changed.

Respond

When the Word of God does its healing, transforming work in us in this way, it calls from us a response which becomes the springboard for our prayer. This response is the third R. It might be a prayer which bursts out as we say our yes to God or as we recognize more fully his love or his greatness or his holiness. It might express the opening up of our heart to God. Or it might result in an outpouring of the love we feel for him, the resolves we want to make or the heart-hunger for him which his Word has exposed.

In time, our response grows. The flow of words ceases. We pass beyond speaking and thinking to "simple presence." "Just being." We become present to the truth or the reality which God has given us.

I recall an occasion when the verse which drew me to itself was: "You renew the face of the earth" (Ps 104:30).

I happened to be sitting in the garden of a cottage in Derbyshire. The day had dawned bright, warm and sunny. The dew hung from the blades of grass like jewels. And I had already written in my prayer journal:

> *Morning has broken like the first morning;*
> *Blackbird has spoken like the first bird.*[11]
>
> *It's that sort of morning and my heart sings and rings your praises*
> *so that it's pure joy to turn to your Word.*

For several minutes, I recited "my" verse: "You renew the face of the earth." And I wrote down the words which came to me: Renew. Make new. Make fresh. Cause to sparkle. Re-fashion. Re-shape.

As I regurgitated "my" verse a prayer burst out of me: "Make me new. Make of my life and my work the freshness which creation rejoices in this morning. Cause me to sparkle for you. Re-fashion and re-shape me. Take every part of my body and perform this miracle with it. May it bring glory to you. I offer back every part of myself to you."

And I began to hum to myself the familiar hymn:

> *Take my life and let it be*
> *Consecrated, Lord, to Thee*
> *Take my moments and my days*
> *Let them flow in ceaseless praise.*[12]

This movement toward God is not rare. Many prayerful people experience it as they respond to God's Word:

> By it God creates in us a greater capacity for himself, not only by our longing but sometimes through the very frustration and powerlessness we experience as we reach out blindly toward him. It is as though we are being drawn by a magnetic force in our own depths, toward God as our center of gravity.[13]

Rest

While we are being drawn toward God in this way, we may find ourselves longing simply to be still: to "be present" to the wonder of God and his creation—resting, relaxing and delighting in his lavish love. "We now not only love (God) but are beginning to 'fall in love'; i.e. he is becoming the realised centre of our lives, and we begin to experience the longing of lovers for union: the desire to be totally given, and totally received."[14] This is the phase of contemplation, the fourth R, when we rest in God, gaze lovingly on him and pay him rapt attention.

Realign: It is while we are gazing on God in this way that the desire to change is re-kindled. We read, not primarily to relish the riches of contemplation, but that we may be continuously converted. Changed. From birth, we live for "number one." Self. But God is concerned to turn us around—to turn us away from narcissistic self-love and self-serving to the self-giving love and service of God and others which Jesus modeled to us. One of the tools he uses to effect these changes is his Word. So when God's Word shows us that we must change in any way, then change we must. Sometimes he shows us that our mind needs to be renewed so that our thoughts are brought into line with his. At other times it is our perception which is challenged and changed until it is brought into alignment with the God of the Bible. And frequently our feelings, desires, lifestyle and attitudes will need to be converted, turned around, so that they become one with his. All he needs is our consent and cooperation. When he has that he, the heavenly potter, will take the raw material of our lives and re-fashion it into a vessel which is more beautiful and more useful than anything we have known previously. This is his ministry.

Pause: *Turn to Isaiah 43:1-24. Apply to these verses the four R's, slipping your own name into the text as seems appropriate.*

Do the same with:
John 15:9-13   Jeremiah 1:4-10
Joshua 1:9   Ephesians 5:8-14
Or listen to the song I gave my life for you *or* My peace *and imagine that these words come from God to you.*

WHEN YOUR WORD GOES FORTH IT GIVES LIGHT

CHAPTER 3

No Part Closed

*I*f we are truly to open ourselves to God we must discover how to open ourselves to his Word, the Bible. That is not because as Christians we are bibliolaters, people who worship a book, but because we worship the God who speaks—and the Bible contains the truths which he has revealed for all time.

In the words of St. Augustine, the Bible is our "letter from home." Or, to use Martin Luther's parables, the Bible is the cradle that bears the Christ to us; this book is like the swaddling clothes in which the infant Jesus was laid: "Poor and mean, are the swaddling clothes, but precious is the Treasure, Christ, that lives therein."[1]

In chapters one and two of this book we examined ways of stilling our minds and bodies in an attempt to be open to God. The reason for this is that silence is to the soul what fertilizer is to the soil—it is preparation for receptivity, growth and fruit-bearing. Just as a seed falling into fertile soil germinates and grows, so God's Word falling into a stilled mind and heart bears fruit.

Donald Coggan puts this persuasively:

There is a power in silence, the very power of God. . . . It is in the silence that the Holy Spirit does his most powerful work, making permanent what otherwise would have been evanescent; impressing truths as a potter makes an impress on clay; register-ing on mind and conscience what has just been said in words.[2]

"Registering on mind and conscience." If God's Word is to register on our mind, we must apply our intellect to the sacred Scriptures. Jesus seems to expect his hearers to do this. Take his parables, for example. They are intellectual teasers, to borrow Peter Toon's phrase. Or take the Sermon on the Mount or the way Jesus describes his kingdom. These, too, invite a series of mental gymnastics.

Paul, similarly, expects his converts not to coast along the road of faith but rather to slip their minds into top gear. To the Romans he writes: "Do not conform outwardly to the standards of this world, but let God transform you inwardly by a complete change of your mind. Then you will be able to know the will of God—what is good, and is pleasing to him, and is perfect" (Rom 12:2 GNB).

· Engaging our minds in this way is not only illuminating and informative; it can be exhilarating too. To embark on a logical, rational meditation of a passage or theme from the Bible so that one emerges with a well-researched, logical conclusion or resolution is both fulfilling and satisfying. Indeed, without such faithful research, we find huge gaps in our understanding of the nature of God and his dealings with men and women.

Think, for example, of the word *heart*. Mention that word to twentieth-century Western Christians and they will think either of the small organ which pumps the blood supply to the human body or to the symbol of love which dominates most Valentine cards. But the Bible refers to "the heart" more than 963 times. Sometimes the word refers to the seat of the emotions, sometimes to the memory, sometimes to the place where we plan, sometimes to our innermost being and sometimes it means the will.

Or take the name Jesus. To the twentieth-century Western Christian a name is the label which distinguishes one person from another. And though there has been a resurgence of interest in the root meaning of certain names, few people take such meanings seriously. Not so the Jews. To them the word *name* included the name-tag "John," "Peter," "Mary," "Rebecca," but it meant far more than that. When they spoke of "the name," they were referring to the entire personality. If we are truly to be open to God, we need to apply our minds so that we unearth such hidden meanings.

Similarly, if we are serious in our quest truly to be open to God, we need to apply our minds to concepts and phrases and words which have been cheapened by our culture, removed from our vocabulary or whose connotations remain hidden to twentieth-century Western Christians.

Take the word *love* for example. It has been so trivialized by the media that we need to ask ourselves certain questions before we can begin to claim that we understand the biblical use of the word. We can do this by looking up the word *love* in a concordance and asking ourselves a series of pertinent questions: What does the Bible mean by love? What is entailed in the practice of love? Why does Jesus exhort us to love one another as he loves us? What is the value of this kind of love? How might I begin to love like that? What aids are there to help me to become more loving? Who are the people in the Bible, in history and in contemporary society who will model this dimension of love to me?

Such objective research always asks a permutation of seven questions: what, why, how, who, where, when, with what helps? Objective research is invaluable, even essential, if we would open ourselves to the God of the Bible.

Pause: *Look up the word* love *in a concordance and attempt to answer the above questions.*

Look up the word faith *and apply the same questions to this word.*

Look up the word money *in a concordance and make a note of the Bible's teaching on this subject. Make a similar study of words which are of particular interest to you.*

For decades now, the church, with its sermons and study groups, its Lenten studies and its prayer groups, has majored on opening the *minds* of the faithful to God. And that, as far as it goes, is vital, as we have seen. But if Christians open only their minds to the Spirit of God, they become rather like the Cheshire cat which appeared to Alice in Wonderland from time to time: a cat with a huge grin and no body.

But a Christian who is a Christian from the neck up or, worse, a Christian who is unaware that there is anything other than the mind to be opened to God, has not begun to understand the God of the Bible who, from earliest times, instructed his people to "love the LORD your God with all your heart and with all your soul and with all your strength" (Deut 6:5).

The *heart*, as we have observed, hides a whole cluster of meanings. According to *The New Bible Dictionary*[3] it means "the centre of things," "the inner man," "the personality," "the inner life," "the spring of all desires," as well as "the memory," "the seat of the will," "the seat of the intellect." In other words, the injunction in this first and great commandment is to love God with our whole person, from the very ground of our being. And that means with our body, mind, memory, emotions, affections, imagination. Everything we have and everything we are must be opened up to God.

The Memory

Everything. That includes opening our memory to God. The command to "remember" is a recurring one both in the Old Testament and the New. "Remember how the LORD your God led you . . . to humble you and to test you in order to know what was in your heart" (Deut 8:2). "Remember . . . what you have received and heard" (Rev 3:3). And, as Peter Toon points out so helpfully:

> At the centre of the annual Passover celebration was the reading of, reflection upon and remembering of the great saving deed of God we call the Exodus. Also at the very centre of the Lord's Supper/Eucharist, the central act of worship of the Church over the centuries, is the remembrance of the mighty act of God in the new Exodus, the great deliverance wrought by God in Christ at Calvary's cross and in resurrection from the power of death.[4]

When we obey this command to remember, we have at our disposal a great potential for openness to God. We all have memories. And our memories work overtime. We play on the screen of our mind the quarrel which upset us, the unkind words that were said about us or the praise people gave us. In a similar way, we can harness our memories to specific examples of God's expressed love for us.

The psalmist seems to have done this regularly. He writes: "I will remember the deeds of the LORD; yes, I will remember your miracles of long ago" (Ps 77:11). And as we do the same, we discover how easy it becomes to imitate the psalmist in another way—by coming into God's presence with thanksgiving. Stored memories of God's love and tenderness also stir up in us a response of love, strengthen us for the present moment and give rise to fresh hope.

Pause: *Spend a few minutes each day recalling the events of the previous twenty-four hours. Select from the video playing in your mind the good gifts God has given you during this period. Thank him for them. Then watch the action replay again. This time observe your moods. Talk to Jesus*

about them and the way you reacted to certain situations and people.
Finally, make a mental note of any ways in which you failed God, yourself
or other people. Ask God to forgive you and to give you the grace to live
differently.

The Imagination

Just as there is value in opening our minds, our memories and our
bodies to God, so whole new vistas open up to us when we engage
our imagination in our contemplation of God. Many people find
this difficult. Some are frightened of their imagination. Others are
embarrassed to admit that they have one. John Powell paints the
picture accurately:

Somehow the same people who believe that God can enter the
mind with his ideas and perspectives, the will with his strength
and desires, or the emotions with his peace, balk at the thought
that God can stimulate the imagination to hear inwardly actual
words or see actual visions. . . . This, of course, was the problem
with Joan of Arc and her voices. The following is a short excerpt
from George Bernard Shaw's play *St. Joan:*

ROBERT: How do you mean. Voices?

JOAN: I hear voices telling me what to do. They come from
God.

ROBERT: They come from your imagination.

JOAN: Of course. That is how the messages of God come to
us.[5]

One reason why the imagination needs to be made available to God
is that it is the key that unlocks the inner world of our personality:
the "heart." "Love the LORD your God with all your heart . . ."

Another reason is that true prayer is a love relationship between the
person praying and God. It follows that the language of this relationship is the language of love—heart to heart. And as Gerard Hughes
puts it: "We find and relate to the true, living and loving God first

with our hearts and only then can we also find him with our minds."[6]

The biblical text substantiates that claim. In its struggle to describe this relationship, it uses picture language. According to St. Paul, God loves us as tenderly as a bridegroom loves his bride (Eph 5). According to the Song of Solomon, he loves us as passionately as the lover loves his beloved. And according to Isaiah and Jesus, his love may be likened to perfect parental love: of the infant, the toddler, the teenager and the adult child.

Our minds cannot fully comprehend these concepts. They need the complementary insights of our senses to cope with such mysteries. As Morton Kelsey puts it: "One must encounter and relate to the Divine Love and one will find that images are needed to describe that experience."[7] Such images come to us through God's gift of the imagination.

The imagination puts vital flesh on the skeleton of objective reasoning. Take, for example, one of Jesus' parables: the Prodigal Son. With our rational minds we can learn from this story a great deal about God, about human nature and the grace of forgiveness. But when, with our imagination, we "become" the spendthrift son moping in the pigsty or the waiting father scouring the landscape for the faintest sign of the returning son, the unquenchable love of God will take root in our hearts and that parable will take on a wealth of new meaning. Our findings will not vie with or challenge the findings of the intellect. They will supplement and complement them in a life-changing way.

Bishop Theophane summed this up beautifully when he wrote: "The principal thing is to stand before God with the intellect in the heart, and to go on standing before him unceasingly day and night, until the end of life." Commenting on this quaint but profound saying, "with the intellect in the heart," Peter Toon observes:

> Standing before God suggests a personal relationship—of child and heavenly Father, of sinner and Saviour, and of servant and Master. Standing before him in the heart suggests an attitude of sincere openness in the very centre of our being, the place where

Love creates love; further, the placing of the intellect (mind) in the heart means that there is no opposition between head and heart, for both are open to, and submitted to, the Lord God.[8]
To submit the intellect and the personality to God. Both are necessary for those who would be radically open to God and mature in Christ.

And Peter Toon reminds us that those who engage the imagination in their contemplation of the Scriptures benefit in other ways. They discover, for example, that they are no longer confined by time or space. When their imagination starts working on a project, they may kneel or lie prostrate on the floor of their prayer place while, at the same time, being in Bethlehem watching Mary place the newborn Christ-child in the manger. A few minutes later, they can be climbing the Mount of Transfiguration with Jesus.

Similarly, this curious gift of the imagination frees us from the restriction of seeing only realities and gives us the ability to "see" absurdities—"a six-legged cow and a four-eyed bird."[9] By fusing images—real legs and real cows—we can create nonsense pictures.

Jesus seems to assume that we will exercise this gift when seeking to understand his teaching. This is the way we enter most fully and creatively into his pen pictures in Luke 6: figs growing on thorn bushes, grapes growing on briars and good fruit growing on rotten trees.

It is possible, of course, to attempt to tease out the reasons why Jesus concocted these strange symbols—but that would be a twentieth-century, Western approach to an Eastern style of teaching. Great Eastern teacher that he was, Jesus appealed to the eye gate and the ear gate more powerfully, in some instances, than to the intellect. He did so expecting his hearers to visualize the incongruities he was describing: clusters of grapes dangling from briars instead of adorning the vine; figs bursting from thorn bushes rather than ripening on the fig tree. Similarly, he expected his hearers to enter into these parables with all their senses: to smell the yeast, to feel it crumbling in their hands, to see the bread rising (Mt 13:33).

In other words, Jesus recognized that, in the imagination, we have a source of knowledge which puts us in touch with hidden realities and offers us ways of relating to them.

Paul, too, persuades us to employ our imagination in our struggle to open ourselves to God and one another. That is why he also uses vivid picture language: the human body, the soldier's armor, clanging gongs and cracked mirrors. This imagery, too, is most powerful if, instead of simply applying our intellect, we so listen to the cacophony made by the noisy gong or clanging bell that we are almost persuaded to place our hands over our ears to shut out the noise.

Imaginative Contemplation of the Scriptures

In *The Celebration of Discipline,* his best-selling book on the spiritual life, Richard Foster stresses the vital contribution the imagination makes to the life of prayer: "The imagination is stronger than conceptual thought and stronger than the will. In the West, our tendency to deify the merits of rationalism—and it does have merit—has caused us to ignore the value of the imagination. . . . Most of us need to be more deeply rooted in the senses."

Foster goes on: "We simply must become convinced of the importance of thinking and experiencing in images. It came so spontaneously to us as children, but for years now we have been trained to disregard the imagination, even to fear it."[10]

Gerard Hughes also emphasizes that the imagination plays a crucial part in the life of the person of prayer. It is the imagination, he claims, which "projects into our conscious minds thoughts, memories and feelings which, although hidden from us in our subconscious, are, in fact, influencing our perception, thinking and acting"[11]—including our perception of God.

This realization—that within the imagination lies the key which unlocks some of the doors which have previously prevented us from being completely open to God—is not new. As long ago as the sixteenth century, St. Ignatius of Loyola recognized it and acted on it, constantly encouraging his retreatants to visualize and enter into the Gospel stories, making maximum use of their senses and feelings as well as their minds and wills. Each of his meditations, the "Spiritual Exercises," as they are best known, assumed the use of the imagination and the five senses.

And just as they revolutionized the lives of countless Christians in the sixteenth century, despite centuries of misuse and disuse, these same meditations have recently re-emerged and are turning the lives of Christians of all denominations and theological persuasions inside-out and upside-down. The chief reason is that once again Christians are being encouraged to engage their God-given nonverbal gifts of sensing and picturing; and in this way they are encountering Christ in the depths of their being. And this is precisely what St. Ignatius intended.

Essential Preparation
The "Spiritual Exercises" have one aim: to strengthen a person's commitment to Christ. This happens most readily not by gritting our teeth and strengthening our resolve but by meeting the living God face to face. Keenly aware of this, St. Ignatius urges us, during our prelude to prayer, to become acutely conscious of whose presence we are entering and of who we are, so that, as we step into our prayer place, we make some gesture which symbolizes our littleness and God's greatness, our sinfulness and God's holiness, our helplessness and God's omnipotence. He suggests, too, that every prayer time should begin with a specific request: that God would turn our whole being to his praise and service.

This advice is invaluable. It encourages us to "center down" immediately and it reminds us of the humbling fact that, even though

we call Jesus "Lord," self very frequently usurps his position. We need, therefore, to be turned away from self and toward him every time we pray.

Beginning to Meditate

When we have prepared and humbled ourselves in the prescribed way, we are almost ready to apply our imagination and senses to the reading of God's Word. But not quite. First, we must read the portion of the Bible we are about to contemplate; St. Ignatius calls this "reading the history of the mystery." The word "mystery" simply means event or story. But as Margaret Hebblethwaite reminds us in her fascinating book *Finding God in All Things*, "The word 'mystery' captures the sense that the events of salvation history do not yield all their truth at the first reading, but contain secret depths."[12]

It is these secret depths that we attempt to plumb with our imagination.

We do this first by reminding ourselves of the historical details, and then by allowing our imagination and senses to roam freely. With our mind's eye and as vividly as possible, we picture the scene.

There are several ways of doing this. Some people find it helpful to imagine that they are trying to describe it for a young child. If they are meditating on the Nativity, they paint a thumbnail sketch of the pregnant mother riding on the donkey, describe the road Mary and Joseph are travelling along and explain what the scenery and the weather are like.

Others find it easier to become a part of the scene for themselves—to imagine that they are walking along beside Mary and Joseph, watching them and listening to their conversation, asking themselves, "What can I see? What do the characters and the scenes look like? What are they saying? What are they doing? What else can I hear?" This can be followed by another soul-searching question: "What can I learn from the people in the picture?" Or "What are my own reactions? What can I learn from them?"

And we make another observation: "Where am I?" In his own meditation on the Nativity, St. Ignatius encourages us to put ourselves into the Nativity drama in a specific way—by imagining not only that we are accompanying Mary and Joseph but that we are their servant. So we travel with them, share in their dismay when they discover that there are no vacancies in the inn, watch Mary giving birth and maybe even assist her.

Those who find themselves becoming actively involved in the scene in this way are advised to take note of their reactions—the little kindnesses with which they express their care for Mary and Joseph, their feelings about being present at the birth, their reactions to the newborn baby:

What have I done practically to make the journey more comfortable for Mary?

How did I feel when we discovered that there was no room in the inn?

How did I react when Mary went into labor?

Where did I go when she was giving birth?

How did I react to the newborn Messiah?

Each person embarking on such an imaginative contemplation, as this method of prayer is often called, will discover unique insights. There is no right or wrong way to do it.

As Gerard Hughes reminds us, "People's imaginative ability varies. Some can imagine with clear pictorial detail and are able to see the size and furnishings of the room, the colour of the walls, the nature of the lighting, the expressions on the faces . . . while others will not see any of these details, the picture being very blurred and indefinite. The details are not important. What is important is that, through the use of our imagination, we should come to know the reality of . . . Jesus."[13]

"To know the reality of Jesus." That for many people is precisely what happens when they begin to meditate on the Gospels in this prescribed way. I think of a priest who confessed, "For years, God for me has been the great unknowable, the Other. But now, thanks to the gift of the imagination, I have encountered him in the depths of my being."

Or I think of a woman who had been praying for years before she discovered the rich resource inside her—her imagination. When she first contemplated the newborn Christ-child in the way I have described, she wept. "I actually saw the Christ-child. I saw his tiny fingers and his outstretched hands. What's more, Mary placed him in my arms. I couldn't believe her generosity. But I held him."

Others similarly have asked, "Can Christmas ever be the same now that I have been present at his birth?" Present at Christ's birth? In one sense of course they were not present. But in another sense, in their imagination, they *have* been there, assimilating the sights and sounds and smells; drinking in, too, that inexpressible wonder:

> *O wonder of wonders that none can unfold,*
> *The Ancient of Days is an Hour or two old.*[14]

And when we have gazed and pondered and adored, we may find a question which Jesus loved to ask of his followers echoing around the labyrinths of our brain: "What do you want?"

We must listen to that question and try to find an honest response to it. As Margaret Hebblethwaite puts it:

> We let Christ question us from out of the mystery we are contemplating: if we are with him in the stable we can let the baby in swaddling clothes challenge us; if we are with him at his Last Supper we can let the Lord who is about to be betrayed turn and put the question; if we are before him on the cross we let the crucified Jesus ask us what we want as we look at him.[15]

And we respond to him in any way which seems appropriate. What

Turn my whole being to your praise & service

often happens in this period of response is that we find ourselves reinforcing in one way or another the prayer of preparation which preceded our meditation:

Turn my whole being to your praise and service.

There is a reason for this. We were loved into being by God and created to enjoy a living relationship with him. As St. Augustine rightly reminds us, our hearts will always be restless until they find their rest in him. And when, using the powerful medium of our imagination, we have seen him and encountered him, we find our heart-yearning for him deepened and strengthened. He becomes, for us, the pearl of great price for whom we would leave everything.

Such is the power of this kind of meditation that we can return to the same Gospel narrative many, many times and still not exhaust its mystery or meaning. Indeed, there is value in taking a series of close-up shots in this way, as well as enjoying the panoramic view.

There is value, too, when we have finished our meditation, in recording what we have seen and heard and felt and learned in a spiritual journal. Some people enjoy this immensely and discover that they pray best at the point of a pen. Others find it more difficult but equally worthwhile. Over a period of weeks and months, we discover that we have a most moving autobiography and a record of the gentle, almost imperceptible nudges God has given us. And these encourage us to journey on in our pilgrimage of prayer which Margaret Hebblethwaite describes so beautifully:

Prayer is something to look forward to beforehand, to relish at the time, and to remember with pleasure afterwards, because prayer is what we choose to do because we love God.[16]

That, most certainly, has been my experience of this kind of prayer both at home and on retreat.

Pause: *The pattern of prayer described in this chapter can be applied to any Gospel story. We:*

1. prepare practically for our imaginative contemplation by making sure that we have a Bible, prayer journal and something to write with in our prayer place.

2. make a deliberate effort to turn our attention in a Godward direction.

3. pray the preparatory prayer, or one which seems similar: "Turn my whole being to your praise and service"—remembering that the word "service" here means relationship as well as servanthood.

4. read "the history of the mystery."

5. set the scene by visualizing it as graphically as possible.

6. hear Jesus say to us from the scene, "What do you want?"; tell him.

7. apply our senses to the story:

    (a) our sight, asking: What can I see? What do the scenes and the characters look like?

    (b) our hearing, asking: What can I hear? What are the characters saying?

    (c) our other senses, asking: What can I smell and feel and taste?

8. ask ourselves:

    (a) Where am I?

    (b) What can I learn from Jesus, the people, from my own reactions?

    (c) What are my reactions? my feelings?

    (d) What do I want to say to the Father, the Son and the Holy Spirit?

9. pray the Lord's Prayer, sometimes listening to it on the tape, or the Anima Christi *(see p. 114).*

10. look back over our experience and write about it in our prayer journal.

11. resolve to come back to this story another day and repeat the exercise.

12. ask that others may be enriched through us as we serve them.

There are times, though, when my imagination refuses to cooperate. At first this used to worry me. But now I realize that such desolation in prayer is both common and valuable, and I am learning how to make the experience work for me.

When I try to meditate in the way I have described and discover that my imagination seems to have gone on strike, I go back over my apparently abortive prayer time and try to recall what I have been doing and thinking. Sometimes I find that I have been turning over in my mind feelings of guilt. At other times I recall how worry about a particular problem has plagued me. And, from time to time, I realize that I have been fingering hurt feelings from which I still smart.

Such moments of insight, I now realize, are gifts of grace. So, instead of trying to force my mind and my imagination to travel along a predetermined path, I use them to bring Jesus into the situations which are so important to me that they have sabotaged my prayer time.

I think, for example, of the occasion when our house had been burgled in broad daylight and fear torpedoed all my attempts to meditate on God's Word. When I abandoned the meditation, gave the fear permission to surface and asked Jesus to come into it, God's love which casts fear out overwhelmed and captivated me.

On other occasions, when my imagination seems to be suffering from a form of paralysis for no reason that I can pinpoint, I use another method of meditation: the four R's which I described in chapter two, or the use of the mind that I underlined at the beginning of this chapter. And it often happens that God will come to me through the intellect instead of through the imagination or the senses. On such occasions I give thanks that God finds a whole host of ways to reveal himself to me.

But there are occasions when meditating on his Word brings, not joy, comfort or consolation but rather utter discomfort.

No consoling word or phrase attracts me to itself. My mind seems sluggish and my imagination seems to have gone to sleep. Meditation seems a waste of time. And I feel confused, betrayed and tempted to give up.

I know
that I am called
   The message was quite clear
   and yet I cannot see
      the how, the why.

I feel so small, so weak,
so ill-equipped
for such a task.

      And yet I am prepared
      to say my YES
   and undertake the risk
   and enter the unknown
   responding to the call.

   Trustfully treading my way
      the only one
   that leads to life — to HIM.

Over the years I have learned to value even these times and to do two things with them. The first is to view them as the activity of the heavenly counsellor, the Holy Spirit; the second is to learn the lessons which can only be learned in the wilderness times.

The Holy Spirit may be likened to the producer of the tape which has been designed to accompany this book. When the singing group was recording a particular song, the harmonies, to me, sounded beautiful. But the skilled, trained, practiced ear of the producer detected a discordant note. "It's the tenors," he announced and replayed the tape to prove his point. When he discovered that he was correct, he insisted that we rerecord the song. His aim, we realized, was not to belittle the tenors but rather to draw out from the entire group their full potential—for their own pleasure and satisfaction as well as for the sake of their ministry.

Similarly, the Holy Spirit's mission is to ensure that every layer of our personality blends as it praises and serves God. He knows that only then will our restlessness be stilled and will we be as effective for Christ as we can possibly be. When one layer of our personality is off-key, he stops us, singles out and even amplifies the failure until we take notice of it. But only so that every part of our being is in tune with God. Harmonious. Enjoying his shalom.

There are times when, although I beg the Spirit to reveal to me the root of my dryness, I hear nothing. Prayer seems empty, God appears to have gone on holiday and meditation produces emptiness rather than fruitfulness. I have learned, during such times, to take heart from Gerard Hughes's claim that the experience of desolation is a good sign, an invitation to grow:

> Desolation will only be experienced by those whose lives are essentially directed to the praise, reverence and service of God. If a person is turned away from God in the core of their being, they may experience the occasional sting of remorse, but in general the felt absence of God will not cause them any pain. . . . If we imagine

ourselves to be in the hands of God as clay in the hands of the potter . . . we can see desolation as a turning of the clay so that it becomes a vessel which can contain life-giving water which as unformed clay it could not hold. Desolation, as it were, gouges us out, so that we can receive more. At the time, the process simply feels painful: when it is over we become aware of new areas of feeling and perception within us.[17]

I have also learned that during such desert experiences I must not do what I feel like doing—abandon prayer and meditation altogether. Rather, I must be prepared to "waste time with God," as some writers on prayer have put it.

Looking back, I recognize that during such times, I probably pray the purest prayer I ever pray. Although I enjoy no peace, no joy, no comfort, no consolation in prayer, my whole being still cries out for God. The certainty inside me grows that it is God himself that I long for—the Giver, not the gifts. Looking back, I know, too, that when God sees that the time is ripe, he will restore that welcome sense of his presence and love once more. Daily prayer, quiet days and retreats will be a delight.

CHAPTER 4

Whole Days to Be Open

*M*editation (that is, memorizing and pondering upon a passage of the Bible or some other spiritual book) and contemplation (that is, gazing at God or one of his creatures) are time-consuming pastimes. For this reason many Christians in the West who, like express trains, rush through life with time to give only a cursory glance at such riches, dismiss these spiritual disciplines as unrealistic, incompatible with the demands of modern life.

But that is not what the person of prayer believes. Quite to the contrary. It often happens that, when the Holy Spirit draws us deeper and deeper into spiritual mysteries, we find within ourselves the desire to carve out of our busy programs whole chunks of time to be quiet so that we may become more open to God. Whenever we do this, whether we realize it or not, we are following in the tradition of the prophets, the patriarchs and of Jesus himself. As Brother Ramon reminds us: "Abraham walked in the desert under the star-filled night. Jacob dreamed in his wilderness solitude at Bethel. . . . And Moses received the revelation and call at the burning bush in the wilderness beneath Horeb."[1]

The New Testament paints a similar picture. There we see John the Baptist spending his entire childhood and adolescence "on retreat" in the desert and Jesus himself spending whole nights under the velvet, star-studded sky in solitary prayer and adoration of his Father. Brother Ramon even claims that "whenever a new chapter opens in God's dealing with people in Scripture, whenever God reveals himself in a new and deeper way, whenever there are moments of revelation, redemption, sanctification—then the person who is the spearhead of such events is called into the mountain, or deep into the desert for confrontation with himself and God."[2]

Even though we may not aspire to the dizzy heights of spearheading or innovating new movements for God, we may still feel drawn to taste for ourselves the elixir of this deep-down, re-creative stillness. We may even clear a space in our diaries to enjoy a Quiet Day, or if we cannot manage a whole day, a regular Quiet Morning, a Quiet Evening or a night-time prayer vigil.

The Value of Quiet Days and Retreats

For the person who desires to deepen his or her relationship with God, this is a wise move because such occasions provide us with the much-needed time and space to make prayer a priority. It also frees us to open up parts of our personality which close automatically when we hurry or when we are bombarded with noise and other stimuli.

This openness is essential for those who are learning to encounter

God through the kind of imaginative contemplation of the Gospels described in chapter three of this book. It is important, too, for people of prayer who want to ruminate in the way described in chapter two. It is also invaluable for anyone who feels drawn to tune in to the multi-level communication which is always coming from the love of God; the communication which comes through our imagination and memory, our emotions and our senses as well as through our mind and our will; the communication which includes that sense of God's presence which most often sweeps over those who have learned to be still.

Time to Contemplate

A Quiet Day also provides us with the space we need to contemplate. Evelyn Underhill likened such days to the experience of visiting a church which is reputed to have magnificent windows:

> Seen from the outside they all look alike—dull, thick, grubby.
> . . . Then we open the door and go inside—leave the outer world,
> enter the inner world—and the universal light floods through the
> windows and bathes us in their colour and beauty and signifi-
> cance, shows us things of which we had never dreamed, a love-
> liness that lies beyond the fringe of speech.

On such days we "contemplate our Christian treasure from inside."[3]

To contemplate our Christian treasure from inside. That sentence, for me, sums up the purpose of a retreat or away day with God. Our most priceless treasure is Christ himself. And on a Quiet Day we have the luxury of leisurely hours, ample space and a variety of aids to help us simply to look up, to conte mplate him.

One such aid might be the meditations outlined in this book. These require time. We need to take at least half an hour for each of them. If we can give ourselves an hour—to read, meditate, pray and write in our prayer journal, so much the better. Even then we shall not have milked them dry. We will find that each time we come back to them they will yield a fresh supply of rich and nourishing insights. Through them we might find answers to some of the questions which were puzzling us before we withdrew from the hurly-burly of the world. And through them we will almost certainly find a new perspective on life—God's perspective. Indeed, the value of a prolonged period of stillness is that we find ourselves viewing life through a different pair of spectacles. God's spectacles.

The story of three bereaved brothers illustrates this simply but powerfully. When their mother died, one of the brothers decided that he would use his pain creatively and announced, "I'm going off to look after the sick. The cities teem with them. I will take them healing and love."

The second brother was equally concerned to be useful. He decided to become one of the world's peacemongers: "Everywhere I go I see people at loggerheads with one another. I'm going out to meet them in their conflict and bring them peace." But the third brother announced, quite calmly, "I'm staying here."

Two years later, the brothers met again for the first time. The first one sighed in despair: "It's useless. There are so many sick people in the world that I can't possibly cope with them all. I can't do all

the things I want to do." The second brother was equally despondent: "It's impossible. I feel torn into tiny shreds. Far from bringing peace to others, I've lost the peace I once had." Whereupon the third brother went to the river and brought back a bowl of muddy water which he stood in the center of the floor.

They watched. And they noticed that gradually the silt sank

to the bottom of the bowl, leaving the water quite clear. That is what happens when people "steal away to Jesus." The silt of their busyness sinks. Their perspective clears. And they hear the still, small voice of God.

Time to Rest

That is not to say that on a Quiet Day we are busy seeking God's guidance all the time. Quiet Days are also occasions for resting in God. Once more we turn to a quotation of Evelyn Underhill's because, although she was writing at the turn of the century before the days of freeways and commuting, of ghetto-blasters and rock groups, no one has put the situation more persuasively:

Our so-called civilisation gets more and more complicated, more and more noisy. It is like one of those mills where the noise of the looms makes it impossible for the workers to hear each other speak. And if we go on at it long enough without a break we begin to think the looms are all that matter, and we are merely there to keep them going and must not bother about anything else.

In other words, I am sure there is a real danger that Christian spirituality in its deepest and loveliest reaches will be killed out by the pressure and demands of the social machines and even of the ecclesiastical machine. Man will get ever more utilitarian and this-worldly and will wholly forget his true relation to God. . . . Even religion tends to become more and more pragmatic, utilitarian; more and more active, and less and less inward; more and more of a chain of doing, less and less of an attachment, a being.

And so by a curious paradox, as man's physical universe gets larger, his true horizon shrinks. He has become a slave of the clattering loom. He can't hear his own soul speak. Now those who control the modern factory . . . know what this means in the exhausting and impoverishing of human material, in nervous tension, apathy, unrest. So there is no good factory without its welfare department, its rest room, its opportunity for quiet. To withdraw the worker from the clatter and pressure is to increase the quantity and quality of the work. So I sometimes think retreats should be regarded as a bit of spiritual welfare work; quite essential to the organisation of the Church, and specially to the efficiency of its ministers. I am sure that were the making of at least a yearly retreat an absolute obligation of the priesthood, this would be a far more direct Way of Renewal than some of those now proposed.[4]

Those words have proved prophetic. People today who live under constant pressure, with continual stress and with ever-increasing noise, need to "duck under," as one nun describes a Quiet Day. To rest. When they do, many discover the kind of prayer Margaret Holliday describes so appetizingly:

the prayer of contemplation, of loving attention to God, the prayer of looking at God, the prayer of being with God, the prayer that needs fewer and fewer words and becomes more and more a relationship. In outward quietness we learn the art of inward quietness. This is a universal kind of prayer and belongs equally to the mystic (St. Teresa has 'eyes grown beautiful with gazing upon God') and the simplest believer singing 'Turn your eyes upon Jesus, look full in his wonderful face.'[5]

Finding a Place

"But where can I go to find the silence necessary for a Quiet Day?" some Christians ask me. There are plenty of possibilities. Some churches may have established Retreat Houses where people can go for such a purpose. Some convents and monasteries also provide rooms which people who want to spend a holiday, literally a holy day with God, can use. The advantage of going to an established house of prayer is that, as soon as you arrive, you tune in to the silence and the rhythm of prayer which permeates the place. You feel engulfed and supported by it. And you can attend the service of Holy Communion which is a daily feature of most such establishments.

But not everyone lives within easy travelling distance of such a prayerful place. In this event, it might be possible to use a friend's cottage or a room in someone else's house. Or, for disciplined people who really are capable of ignoring the chores, the telephone or the papers which beg to be cleared from the desk, one's own prayer place could be used. The secret is to be alone and to turn away from the demands which normally pressurize us.

"To be alone." Some people like to spend their times of quiet on their own, but others prefer to spend a Quiet Day with a group of like-minded people. There are advantages in joining in a group "away day." One woman helped me to recognize afresh the value of the Quiet Days which are organized by many Retreat Houses and churches. This woman told me that she had cleared an entire day and gone away to a nearby convent for what she imagined would be a wonderful experience of prayer. But when she arrived, she realized that she was totally unprepared for such a day.

"I went into the chapel and knelt down to pray. I seemed to have been praying for hours. But when I looked at my watch, I had been there for just ten minutes. And then panic set in. I still had another eight hours to spend in that place. How on earth was I to fill the time?" On an organized Quiet Day, people are relieved from this kind of pressure because the program is carefully pre-planned by the retreat giver. It usually follows this kind of pattern:

10:00 A.M.   Arrive, coffee, welcome
10:30 A.M.   Devotional talk given by the retreat giver
11:00 A.M.   Time for reflection, personal prayer, reading or a chat with the retreat giver for anyone who would like to discuss his or her prayer pilgrimage
12:30 P.M.   Lunch

1:30 P.M.	Another devotional address given by the retreat giver
2:00 P.M.	Another period of reflection, reading, personal prayer or time for a walk
3:00 P.M.	Communion
3:30 P.M.	Refreshments
4:00 P.M.	Depart

Lunch might be sandwiches, a cooked meal or a picnic which the retreatants bring with them. The meal might be eaten in silence; this is not as embarrassing as some people imagine. For most people it even comes as a relief.

One reason for this is that there is no need to make conversation so everyone can relax with their own thoughts and even hear God speak over lunch. Another is that, in the absence of chatter, most people are far more attentive to the needs of the others—passing the salt or the water or the butter without being asked, leaving the others feeling cherished. And, of course, there is the added bonus that, in the absence of jokes and storytelling, each retreatant has the leisure to savor and appreciate the good, wholesome food which is God's gift to us, the music which might be played or the book which might be read during this particular period of stillness.

Using the Time

"But I never seem to be free when these Quiet Days are organized! And yet I do want to discipline myself to spend a whole day with God each month. How should I use the time?"

That is a question I am asked over and over again. It is a difficult question to answer in a book because there is no blueprint for spending a Quiet Day. So much depends on what we need at any particular time. However, there are some guidelines which people seem to find helpful. I include them here with the reminder that all the teachers of prayer emphasize that *we must pray as we can and not try to pray as we can't*. In other words, the guidelines are no more than suggestions. Some will be right for some readers on some occasions but not on others. Others will appeal to other pray-ers on one Quiet Day but may lose their appeal on another day. We must therefore be selective.

Relax

The first guideline is vital. Relax.

Most of us arrive at our chosen hideaway harassed and tense. The need to unwind is urgent. That is one reason why, if there is a choice, a place with a spacious garden, access to the countryside or a stretch of beach might be selected. The Quiet Day can then begin by settling into the room which is to be home for the day, followed almost immediately by a stroll outside where the stillness or the noise of creation almost shrieks at us—the chatter of birds, the surge of the sea, the howling of wind—where nature's magnificence will persuade us to begin to let go of the pressures and anxieties and to drop anchor into God.

This letting go is imperative. While our minds spin like tops and while we clutch in our hands and hearts the problems that perplex and puzzle us, we shall never be completely open to God. But when we have allowed the pressures and tensions to fall off us like snow sliding from the rooftops in the thaw, we find ourselves ready to receive each and every word God speaks to our listening hearts.

We unwind while we walk and while we enjoy a leisurely cup of tea or listen to music. By this time, we may feel prepared in body, mind and spirit to read one or two paragraphs from a book about prayer before turning to a passage from God's Word, the Bible.

Meditate

The earlier chapters of this book contain several suggestions for drinking in God's Word. A Quiet Day is a good time to experiment with these and to discover which work at this moment in time. Some will find that reading a passage and applying the four R's described in chapter two will exactly meet their need on a particular day.

Others will feel more prepared to do a thematic study of a particular word or phrase of Scripture using the questions listed in chapter three. Yet others will rejoice to have the leisure to involve themselves in the kind of imaginative contemplation which is also outlined in chapter three. Or a Quiet Day would be an excellent time to try one or more of the meditations from this book.

Such meditation and contemplation of the Scriptures could take at least an hour, by which time it will be important to take a break of some kind. We cannot meditate or pray all the time. Human beings are rather like rubber bands in the sense that if they are over-stretched they break. So we return to guideline number one: relax.

This next phase of relaxation might again be taken in the garden or the countryside, in a nearby park or on the beach where we could enjoy an awareness walk. An awareness walk is a walk where we look for signs of God's presence and personality in the things that he has made. Even if we spend our "away day" in the center of a city, signs of God's presence are scattered around us.

On an awareness walk, we look for such signs and talk to God as we walk: "How powerful you must be, O Lord, if you can cause such gigantic waves to crash against the cliffs in this way; how lovely you must be if you can make such color and splash it around your world so liberally and so generously; how gentle you must be if you can create such kind and gentle people and bring them across my path just when I need them most—if you create these gentle waves which seem to tickle the seashore."

Or this second phase of relaxation might take another, more creative form. For example, I try to carve out time for a Quiet Day each month. This includes a day as soon after Christmas as possible and another day immediately after Easter. The theme of my meditations on these days might be the visit of the Magi or one of the resurrection appearances of Jesus.

So I take with me a scrapbook or a cheap photograph album and a pile of Christmas cards or Easter cards. From the pile, I select the ones which illustrate most effectively the passage of Scripture I am contemplating, and I stick these into my book. I then take time to savor each card—to enjoy it and to ask myself what the artist might have seen and been trying to express by depicting the Gospel scene in this particular way. Underneath the picture, I write or type a relevant passage of Scripture, one of the sayings of the Early Fathers, or a quotation from a book or hymn.

INTO YOUR HANDS, LORD, I COMMEND MY SPIRIT

Some people like to sketch or paint, or to mold lumps of clay. Others like to knit or sew, to help with the gardening or sweep up leaves. Working with one's hands can be very restful. I once took some mending on one of my Quiet Days and enjoyed the creativity of making broken things whole again while I soaked up the stillness. It was the most enjoyable experience of mending I have ever had!

If the day is being spent in a convent or a monastery, lunch will almost certainly be eaten in the kind of delicious silence I have already described. After that, it is time for another rest. Scientists have proved that the body begs to rest for half an hour or so at midday, so after lunch is a good time to spend some "lap time" with God.

By "lap time" I mean the method of prayer St. Teresa taught her nuns. She used to suggest to them that they sit on the floor beside a chair and imagine that Jesus was sitting on the chair. They would then place their head on the chair and imagine that it was resting in the lap of Christ.

Some people find this a comforting and moving way in which to relax. Others find that their imagination will not stretch that far. Yet others are afraid to try it lest they should fall asleep. That is a pity. We need never be frightened of falling asleep when we pray. If we are so tired that we need to snooze we can accept sleep as God's gift to us, nod off and wake up refreshed and ready for a fresh touch from him. He might even speak to us through a dream.

Look Up

By the afternoon, we will probably find that we have unwound, enjoyed meditating on God's Word and we will want simply to look up, to contemplate Christ. Most of the meditations in this book are designed to bring us to the point where our gaze and attention and love and adoration are focused simply on him, so the afternoon is a good time to embark on one of the imaginative contemplations outlined in this book.

Or a Jesuit priest suggests another way of turning our thoughts Godward, of looking up. His method comes in five stages:

Be there with Him and for Him—giving your full attention and concentration.

Want Him. Hunger for Him. Prepare for His coming and His word, as you would want and eagerly prepare for a visit with the dearest person in your life. Invite Him to reveal and communicate Himself to you, to speak to you and teach you how to listen deeply to Him.

Listen to Him with faith deeply and reverently; listen with trust; listen with hunger to be fed by His word; listen with gratitude and in peace, with searching for hidden meanings. Forget about implications, applications, conclusions, resolutions. Be simple, like a child nestled in its father's lap, peacefully listening to his story.

Let Him be with you. Let Him be for you what He wants to be. Let Him love you. Let Him speak to you. Let Him hold you and console you and forgive and strengthen you. Let Him take you through dryness and darkness, if He prefers—but let Him. What Jesus wants, Jesus deserves. Trust yourself to Him. Let Him be for you. Let Him fill you afresh with His Spirit. Let Him become more and more alive and real to you.

Respond to Him in any way you want to or feel moved to respond. Be genuinely yourself and respond honestly, freely, spontaneously, reverently. Speak what is in your heart; say what you feel, even when you feel like complaining. Remember that when you don't know what to say, the Holy Spirit prays in you and for you. Just speaking or whispering the name of Jesus rhythmically with your breathing, or repeating words of praise and thanks, are profoundly prayerful responses.[6]

Look In

Having looked up to express our confidence and trust in God, we can then look in.

One of the most effective ways I know of doing this without falling into the trap of excessive introspection is to take Jesus' invitation seriously: "Behold, I stand at the door and knock; if any one hears my voice and opens the door, I will come in" (Rev 3:20 RSV). So we use our imagination and open the door of our lives to him.

We notice, in passing, whether, when we hear his knock, we throw open the door in welcome or exasperation or gingerly from reluctance, despair, fear or awe. When we feel we are ready, we invite him inside. But instead of leaving him standing in the hall we suggest that we go on a tour of the house together. We take him into one room at a time, noticing in passing which rooms we are happy for him to inspect and which rooms we shall enter with reluctance or shame. Maybe we even clutch in our hands the key of a room which we shall keep firmly locked for some reason?

But inside the rooms we do enter with him, we notice his reaction as he surveys the decor and the furnishings, the structure and the design. We notice, too, whether he comments on the atmosphere which permeates the place. And we remind ourselves that Love is what he is—the love which is patient and kind, gentle and anxious that the loved one always enjoys the best. So at the end of the tour, we sit down with him to listen carefully to his suggestions.

We then tell him that our home is his home and we invite him, not only to make the necessary changes to the fabric and atmosphere, but to invite into the home the guests of his choice. We listen while he tells us who those people are.[7]

Another way of looking in objectively and responsibly is to ask ourselves a series of questions:

Does anything in my life stand between God and me?

Is anything preventing me from giving myself freely to fulfill
God's plan for my life?
What have I been doing for God?
What am I doing for him at present?
What would I like to do for him?
What do I sense he is asking of me?

Look Out
We ask these questions because a successful retreat or Quiet Day
always has an impact on others. That is why I almost always suggest
to my retreatants at some stage of their time away from home that
they draw a diagram which looks like this:

The large dot represents oneself. The smaller dots arranged around
the semicircle represent those with whom we live and work and worship, and our neighbors and friends. At various stages of the retreat,
I suggest that we recollect what God is saying to us and we begin to
try to discern how we can translate this into a language or way of life
which will benefit these people. This is of vital importance. For a
retreat or Quiet Day must never be simply an escape from the world.
Rather, it must always be a withdrawal with a purpose: that our energy
level be topped up and our will so brought into alignment with God's
that we go out reinvigorated to touch and to bless the lives of others.

That is why, when we are on retreat, much of our thinking and
discovering will be mundane rather than mystical. Richard Foster
warns us to expect this:

Often meditation will yield insights that are deeply practical, almost mundane. There will come instruction on how to relate to

your wife or husband, on how to deal with this sensitive problem or that business situation. More than once I have received guidance on what attitude to have when lecturing in a college classroom. It is wonderful when a particular meditation leads to ecstasy, but it is far more common to be given guidance in dealing with ordinary human problems.[8]

Perhaps that is why a certain husband, on learning from his wife that she planned to go on retreat for a few days, took his pipe from his mouth and agreed readily: "Go, my dear. Go, by all means! You're just about due for a spot of re-birth."[9]

"A spot of re-birth." When we are on retreat it sometimes seems as though we are re-born. As we look up, we find ourselves cherished and suckled. As one young man expressed it: "I feel as though I have been guzzling at the breast of God." We look in and, with characteristic gentleness, the heavenly potter points out the flaws before reshaping, remolding and refilling us. We look out and our compassion for God's world and its people is so rekindled that we go back to it as bearers of the light and love of Christ—pregnant with Christ, as one person has put it. New.

Annual Retreats

It often happens that, even when people of prayer set aside a regular time of quiet each day and a Quiet Day each month, they still pant for more stillness. An annual retreat then becomes not a luxury but a necessity. And a whole variety of such retreats are available.

The traditional form of retreat, the *preached retreat,* is still very popular. These usually take place at a convent, a monastery or a Retreat House. They are led by a retreat conductor who gives a series of short devotional talks which fuel prolonged periods of reflection and private prayer. The retreat givers also make themselves available to talk about the pilgrimage of prayer with retreatants who would welcome the opportunity.

PREPARATION FOR PRAYER ✚

Before you go into your place of prayer, remember to 'tune your instrument at the gate'.

Always approach your prayer place with reverence and awe, and just before you settle into it, make some small gesture which reminds you that you are about to meet with the King of Kings and Lord of Lords:

....Kneel in silence....

...or stand reverently

...or light a candle....

...or make the sign of the cross.

...or gaze at a favourite picture which reminds you of JESUS

REMAIN QUITE STILL

BE AWARE OF GOD'S PRESENCE
RELAX IN IT
DRINK IN HIS LOVE

LOOK BACK OVER THE PAST TWENTY-FOUR HOURS. CONCENTRATE ON AND GIVE THANKS TO GOD FOR EVERY SIGN OF HIS GOODNESS AND LOVE WHICH YOU SEE UNFOLDING ON THE SCREEN OF YOUR MIND.

But increasing in popularity are *experiential retreats* where retreat givers encourage retreatants to use not just their minds but their bodies, their feelings, their senses and their imagination in the three-fold discipline of looking up, looking in and looking out which I have described. *Adventure retreats* are for those for whom prolonged silence is a new experience but who long to experiment with it in the safety of a group and with the security of experienced leaders.

Journaling retreats are silent workshops aiming to help retreatants make the best possible use of the spiritual journal.

Individually guided retreats, based on the Spiritual Exercises of St. Ignatius, last for between six and thirty days with each retreatant meeting with a retreat giver daily to discuss the outcome of the imaginative contemplations which occupy most of the day.

Drop-in retreats are becoming more and more popular. These retreats are non-residential and may extend over a period of several days. Each day is structured to include talks, meditations, silence and the opportunity for personal prayer. Its main aim is to make available a holy space for those whose commitments prevent them from going into retreat in the traditional way. As such, they are extremely valuable.

And so are *home retreats.* In my own city, we once experimented with a directed home retreat. It was given by four people and there were sixteen retreatants who all continued with their teaching or nursing or traveling or homemaking duties while they were on the week-long retreat. The week began with a meeting for the entire group when the structure was explained and when one of the retreat givers led an imaginative contemplation of a Gospel story. All the retreatants had committed themselves to spend at least half an hour in prayer each day and to a daily half-hour session with their retreat giver. They were introduced to their retreat giver after this initiatory plenary session.

At the end of the session, they were each given a passage of

Scripture on which to base their first prayer time. Next day, when they met with their retreat giver, they explained, as best they could, what had arisen during their half-hour of prayer. They had been forewarned that the retreat giver's role was not to offer counseling or prayer ministry but simply "to listen to the base line," to borrow Michael Jacob's phrase, and to attempt to assess what was going on between the retreatant and God. After a brief time of discussion, the retreat giver gave the retreatant a passage of Scripture or a Gospel story on which to base his or her meditation for the next prayer phase.

The results of this week of guided prayer exceeded all our expectations. Although we were not offering prayer for healing or specific prayer for anything, we watched retreatants make significant moves into degrees of wholeness they scarcely dared dream of. It was as though we had witnessed for ourselves a claim Thomas Merton once made: "It is in silence and not in commotion, in solitude and not in crowds that God best likes to reveal himself most intimately to men." And women!

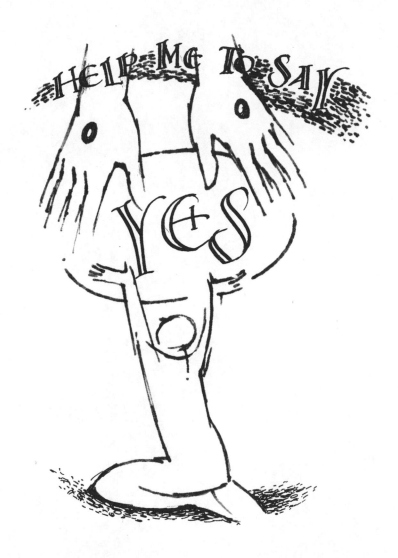

Behold the handmaid of the Lord

Be it unto me according to your Word —

M E D I T A T I O N 1

Help Me to Say Yes . . .
to Any Request

N ew beginnings with God often take place in ordinary,
even domestic settings. Luke records the momentous
new beginning which happened for Mary when the an-
gel Gabriel came to visit her. Before we read about this mysterious
appearance of God's messenger, we pray slowly and meditatively:

God of love and mercy,

help us to follow the example of Mary,

always ready to do your will.[1]

Reading

We read Luke 1:26-38:

In the sixth month, God sent the angel Gabriel to Nazareth, a town in Galilee, to a virgin pledged to be married to a man named Joseph, a descendant of David. The virgin's name was Mary. The angel went to her and said, "Greetings, you who are highly favored! The Lord is with you."

Mary was greatly troubled at his words and wondered what kind of greeting this might be. But the angel said to her, "Do not be afraid, Mary, you have found favor with God. You will be with child and give birth to a son, and you are to give him the name Jesus. He will be great and will be called the Son of the Most High. The Lord God will give him the throne of his father David, and he will reign over the house of Jacob forever; his kingdom will never end."

"How will this be," Mary asked the angel, "since I am a virgin?"

The angel answered, "The Holy Spirit will come upon you, and the power of the Most High will overshadow you. So the holy one to be born will be called the Son of God. Even Elizabeth your relative is going to have a child in her old age, and she who was said to be barren is in her sixth month. For nothing is impossible with God."

"I am the Lord's servant," Mary answered. "May it be to me as you have said." Then the angel left her.

Reflection

We are not told what Mary was doing when the angel appeared to her. What we are told is that she was an ordinary peasant girl who was probably not more than fourteen years old. It is most likely that this ordinary girl was performing ordinary domestic duties when God sent his messenger to her. And in one sense what God asked of her was also very ordinary. He simply invited her to continue with the plans which had already been made for her—to marry Joseph.

Outwardly her life would not change. But inwardly, in the secret places of her innermost being, as she surrendered to God the gift of her ordinary, everyday life and the gift of her humanity, mysterious and awesome changes would take place. He would infuse this ordinariness with his own divine energy and presence which, for Mary, would come in the form of the divine fetus: the actual presence of Jesus. "It seemed that God wanted to give the world the impression that it is ordinary for Him to be born of a human creature."[2]

But the seed of the Son of God would not have been planted in Mary's womb without her willingness and self-surrender. God does not force himself or his gifts on anyone. He waited for her yes. When she uttered it, the momentous new beginnings which were to change the direction of her entire life seemed almost effortless:

> *She was not asked to do anything for herself, but to let something be done to her. She was not asked to renounce anything, but to receive an incredible gift.*[3]

Just as God needed all that Mary had and all that she was to rescue our world from destruction, so he needs us: our souls and bodies, our talents and possessions, our humanity and our ordinariness And just as he gave the incredible gift of his own life to Mary, so he longs to impregnate us with divine energy and power. But he needs our yes.

We reread Luke 1:26-38.

We imagine that we are in heaven with the Father, the Son and the Holy Spirit before the birth of Jesus. We look down on the whole expanse of earth and see it teeming with human beings. Some enjoy peace and plenty, others suffer the ravages of war, deprivation and starvation; some are laughing, others are weeping; some are millionaires, others are homeless. All are hurtling to disaster. And we hear the Holy Trinity decide that "the fullness of time has come" for the Son to leave the splendors of heaven and to come to earth to rescue mankind.

We imagine the three members of the Godhead searching for someone on earth who would be willing and capable of caring for God's

Son in the formative years of his infancy and adolescence; someone capable of bringing him up in a way which would enable him to mature in the way God always intended. We watch the world revolve, like the familiar globe we sometimes see on television, and we notice that their gaze focuses on the tiny town of Nazareth—and on Mary.

As we watch, God sends his special envoy, the angel Gabriel, to Mary and we picture him; we listen to the nuances of the questions he asks and the responses Mary makes. We notice the expression on Mary's face, the look in her eyes and the gestures and movements which tell so much about a person. We spend as many moments as we can spare simply gazing at the scene as it unfolds—contemplating the mystery.

Response

We ask ourselves: Where have I been in my imagination and how do I want to respond?

We make no attempt to use all the ideas suggested here. We simply use the ones which we are attracted to. Our response is leisurely. We enjoy receiving and lingering over God's good gift to us. But we might want to ask ourselves a series of questions:

What can I learn from Mary?

And what do I learn from the quiet, simple way in which God works?

What emotions have surfaced and how have I reacted while I have been immersing myself in the mystery?

It sometimes helps to record these insights in a notebook reserved for the purpose—a prayer journal.

We pray (perhaps in writing) to the Father, the Son and the Holy Spirit separately.

Or we listen to the track on the tape: *Lord, you gave me everything,* making the words our own.[4]

Speak, Lord, your servant is listening...

LORD, turn my whole being to your praise and service

MEDITATION 2

Help Me to Say Yes . . .
When Weary or Worried

S ome people seem to be under the impression that listening to God is women's work. But the Bible persuades us that God speaks just as clearly and incisively to men as to women. Think of Joseph, Mary's fiance, for example. Matthew, in whom Joseph must surely have confided at some stage, presents us with a moving cameo of the way God broke into this man's anxiety to give him precise and much-needed guidance.

We pray the prayers of Samuel and of St. Ignatius:

Speak, Lord, your servant is listening.
Lord, turn my whole being to your praise and service.

Reading
We read Matthew 1:18-25:

> *This is how the birth of Jesus Christ came about: His mother Mary was pledged to be married to Joseph, but before they came together, she was found to be with child through the Holy Spirit. Because Joseph her husband was a righteous man and did not want to expose her to public disgrace, he had in mind to divorce her quietly.*
>
> *But after he had considered this, an angel of the Lord appeared to him in a dream and said, "Joseph son of David, do not be afraid to take Mary home as your wife, because what is conceived in her is from the Holy Spirit. She will give birth to a son, and you are to give him the name Jesus, because he will save his people from their sins."*
>
> *All this took place to fulfill what the Lord had said through the prophet: "The virgin will be with child and will give birth to a son, and they will call him Immanuel"—which means, "God with us."*
>
> *When Joseph woke up, he did what the angel of the Lord had commanded him and took Mary home as his wife. But he had no union with her until she gave birth to a son. And he gave him the name Jesus.*

Reflection
We imagine that we are one of Joseph's closest friends. Today, as we saunter down the narrow, cobbled streets of Nazareth, we step into his workshop for a chat. As we enter the small cave in which he works, we smell the scent of the wood shavings, notice the carpenter's tools lying around and finger some of Joseph's handiwork. But when we see our friend's face, we find, not the normal cheery craftsman who has endeared himself to the entire village, but rather a morose and worried man. He pours out his troubles, telling how he discovered that Mary was pregnant. He expresses his fears for

her, his hurt, anger, shock and bewilderment. And we detect that, now that his hopes for the future have been dashed to tiny pieces, his world seems to have fallen apart.

Joseph discusses with us the options open to him: to divorce Mary publicly, running the risk of ruining her reputation and endangering her life—or to break off the engagement privately, protecting her from the possible punishment of public stoning. While he talks, the numbness wears off and he reaches his resolve: to break off the engagement quietly.

The next day, we visit Joseph again. We listen while he describes the dream which has persuaded him to marry Mary after all! We take careful note of the phraseology the angel used, calling Joseph "son of David" as though to convince him that the Messiah was to be one of his descendants.

We notice, too, how Gabriel entrusts to Joseph the child's name and, by implication, the responsibility of the fatherly role of pronouncing that name at the circumcision ceremony. We help Joseph to perceive that his vocation is as vital to God's plan as Mary's. Joseph senses the urgency of marrying Mary as quickly as possible, and he asks us to help him with the preparations.

Response

We walk away from his shop with a whirl of impressions tumbling around in our minds. As we tramp the narrow, cobbled streets of Nazareth, we relive the experiences of the past two days, reminding ourselves of what we have seen and heard and felt and sensed.

We refuse to hurry, bearing in mind that our best, most honest response will probably come slowly and gradually. We relish one insight at a time, receiving from it everything God wants us to receive without any eagerness to go on until we have been nourished. We recall how we felt about Joseph when we first encountered him—worried and downhearted. We reflect on the change in him and ask ourselves, "What can I learn from him?" and "What can I learn from this God who has given him such clear and specific instructions?"

We make our own response to God, either in writing or by saying a prayer or remaining quiet in his presence. Or we worship him using *To love only you* or *The Lord's Prayer* from the tape. We hold in our mind's eye the picture we have seen of the anxious lines on Joseph's face and we gather into our prayers all who, today, are in any kind of anguish or despair. We ask God to show us whether there is anything he would have us do to alleviate the suffering of some of them.

MEDITATION 3

Help Me to Say Yes . . .
When Disappointed or Elated

Yesterday, we placed the spotlight on Joseph and saw that God speaks as clearly to men as to women. Today we watch God intervene in the life of a married couple and observe how, once again, it was the husband to whom God spoke clearly and directly.

But first we pray a prayer of the psalmist:

Open my eyes, O Lord, that I may behold wonderful things from your Word.

Reading

Luke records the wonderful way in which God made his plans plain to a godly couple: the priest Zechariah and his elderly wife, Elizabeth. We read about it in Luke 1:5-25:

In the time of Herod king of Judea there was a priest named Zechariah, who belonged to the priestly division of Abijah; his wife Elizabeth was also a descendant of Aaron. Both of them were upright in the sight of God, observing all the Lord's commandments and regulations blamelessly. But they had no children, because Elizabeth was barren; and they were both well along in years.

Once when Zechariah's division was on duty and he was serving as priest before God, he was chosen by lot, according to the custom of the priesthood, to go into the temple of the Lord and burn incense. And when the time for the burning of incense came, all the assembled worshipers were praying outside.

Then an angel of the Lord appeared to him, standing at the right side of the altar of incense. When Zechariah saw him, he was startled and was gripped with fear. But the angel said to him: "Do not be afraid, Zechariah; your prayer has been heard. Your wife Elizabeth will bear you a son, and you are to give him the name John. He will be a joy and delight to you, and many will rejoice because of his birth, for he will be great in the sight of the Lord. He is never to take wine or other fermented drink, and he will be filled with the Holy Spirit even from birth. Many of the people of Israel will he bring back to the Lord their God. And he will go on before the Lord, in the spirit and power of Elijah, to turn the hearts of the fathers to their children and the disobedient to the wisdom of the righteous—to make ready a people prepared for the Lord."

Zechariah asked the angel, "How can I be sure of this? I am an old man and my wife is well along in years."

The angel answered, "I am Gabriel. I stand in the presence of God, and I have been sent to speak to you and to tell you this good news.

And now you will be silent and not able to speak until the day this happens, because you did not believe my words, which will come true at their proper time."

Meanwhile, the people were waiting for Zechariah and wondering why he stayed so long in the temple. When he came out, he could not speak to them. They realized he had seen a vision in the temple, for he kept making signs to them but remained unable to speak.

When his time of service was completed, he returned home. After this his wife Elizabeth became pregnant and for five months remained in seclusion. "The Lord has done this for me," she said. "In these days he has shown his favor and taken away my disgrace among the people."

Reflection

Israel was well endowed with priests at this stage of its history, and so the priestly privilege of entering the Holy of Holies came but once in a lifetime. Luke takes up his story on the day when Zechariah's turn had come; when he was about to enter this inner sanctuary to burn incense and to pray, on behalf of the people of Israel, that the Messiah would soon come.

It is probable that Zechariah added to this national prayer a private one: that God would give the gift of a child to his wife, for she was childless and this brought the couple a double sorrow: the stigma of barrenness for Elizabeth and the disappointment for Zechariah that he would have no descendants.

Every afternoon, when the priest on duty entered the awesome Holy of Holies, a great crowd of worshipers would gather in the temple precincts to pray. We imagine that we are a part of that crowd and that we have been selected from it and granted the unprecedented privilege of accompanying Zechariah into this holy place where normally only priests are allowed to tread. We help him prepare the incense before retreating to a corner to wait and watch. We see the visiting angel and hear his voice. We also hear and see

Zechariah's response. We ask ourselves:

How does it feel to be in this prayer-saturated place—the Holy of Holies?

What can I see and hear and smell?

What is Zechariah doing?

How does he pray? Silently? With words? With his body?

How does he seem to be feeling? What happens when the angel comes? What does he do? What does he say? Do any particular words lodge in my mind? What are they?

We gaze at this expression of God's lavish love for as long as we can. But when Zechariah leaves the Holy of Holies, we leave with him. We notice whether this elderly priest needs our support or whether he has been re-energized and rejuvenated by the vision he has just seen.

We take a careful look at the crowd as we reappear with Zechariah. We scrutinize, too, the priest's face and figure. And we observe the crowd: their realization that God has appeared to Zechariah, the awe with which they greet him. We notice, too, what gestures he makes to try to communicate to them what has happened.

Response

We reflect on our surroundings, asking ourselves: What have I learned from Zechariah? And what has the experience taught me about God? Where have I been during this meditation? Have I been an onlooker? Or did I "become" Zechariah? Have I been intimately involved or distant and objective? There is no right or wrong but

it helps to be aware. What have I been doing and feeling and de-
siring? What do I want God to do for me? We tell him. Or we listen
to the Taize chant *My peace* as we seek from God the assurance the
angel gave to Zechariah: "Your prayer has been heard." We hold in
our mind's eye the picture of the aging priest praying for the gift
of a child, and we gather into that mental picture the many couples
who remain childless today. Or we simply ponder on the mysteries
we have seen and heard and felt and experienced in our imagination.

Or we write or say a prayer asking, perhaps, that we might not
simply be open to God but that we might believe him when he does
reveal himself.

We pray:
Open my eyes, O Lord,
that may see the chariots of fire,
and the crowd of watching angels and saints,
the four living creatures of creation,
the hosts of the redeemed,
from every nation and every generation,
and thyself standing in the place of power,
directing thy Kingdom
and strengthening every struggling follower.
So seeing thee,
may I be held quiet and unafraid,
ready and daring, to be and do and bear
all that thy loving wisdom allows or wills,
O beloved Author and Finisher of my faith.[1]

MEDITATION 4

Help Me to Say Yes . . .
Even When Doubting

A group of young people was once asked the question, "Do you think God understands radar?" Almost all of them instinctively said no. They then laughed as their conscious minds realized the absurdity of their answer and recognized that, subconsciously, they believed in a God whose ability to cope with a technological age was inadequate.

But as J. B. Phillips reminds us: "We can never have too big a conception of God, and the more scientific knowledge (in whatever field) advances, the greater becomes our idea of His vast and complicated wisdom."[1]

Even so, most of us struggle truly to believe in this all-powerful God we worship. Real faith sets reservations, doubts and misgivings aside and takes God at his word when he says that he loves us. Real faith goes further. It stakes its life on the trustworthiness and promises of God. And real faith affects not just the mind. Real faith leaves no area of our life untouched. Is it any wonder that people of real faith are few and far between; that when God discerns one he applauds and honors that one? But such is God's love for us that he woos to himself *not* just those who expect that he really will fulfill all his promises; God also draws to himself the doubters, those whose faith is no bigger than a mustard seed.

Reading

Luke does not hide the fact that Zechariah was a reluctant believer while Mary, like the illustrious list of believers mentioned in Hebrews 11, seems to have been given an enviable ability to trust: to allow God to be God. Neither does Luke hide the fact that God blessed richly both Zechariah and his wife, Elizabeth. We read about this in Luke 1:57-80.

When it was time for Elizabeth to have her baby, she gave birth to a son. Her neighbors and relatives heard that the Lord had shown her great mercy, and they shared her joy.

On the eighth day they came to circumcise the child, and they were going to name him after his father Zechariah, but his mother spoke up and said, "No! He is to be called John."

They said to her, "There is no one among your relatives who has that name."

Then they made signs to his father, to find out what he would like to name the child. He asked for a writing tablet, and to everyone's astonishment he wrote, "His name is John." Immediately his mouth was opened and his tongue was loosed, and he began to speak, praising God. The neighbors were all filled with awe, and throughout the hill country of Judea people were talking about all these things. Everyone who heard this wondered about it, asking, "What then is this child going to be?" For the Lord's hand was with him.

His father Zechariah was filled with the Holy Spirit and prophesied:

"Praise be to the Lord, the God of Israel,
*   because he has come and has redeemed his people.*
He has raised up a horn of salvation for us
*   in the house of his servant David*
(as he said through his holy prophets of long ago),
salvation from our enemies
*   and from the hand of all who hate us—*
to show mercy to our fathers
*   and to remember his holy covenant,*
*   the oath he swore to our father Abraham:*
to rescue us from the hand of our enemies,
*   and to enable us to serve him without fear*
*   in holiness and righteousness before him all our days.*

And you, my child, will be called a prophet of the Most High;
*   for you will go on before the Lord to prepare the way for him,*
to give his people the knowledge of salvation
*   through the forgiveness of their sins,*
because of the tender mercy of our God,
*   by which the rising sun will come to us from heaven*
to shine on those living in darkness
*   and in the shadow of death,*
to guide our feet into the path of peace."

And the child grew and became strong in spirit; and he lived in the desert until he appeared publicly to Israel.

Reflection

In our imagination we travel to the hill country near Nazareth eight days after the birth of the baby John, who will come to be called John the Baptist. We attend the circumcision ceremony when the baby is named. We see for ourselves the elderly parents of the child and listen while the priests and relatives and neighbors make the assumption that the baby will be named after his father. We hear Elizabeth assert that the infant's name is to be John. And we watch while the crowd protests and, using sign language, puts the question of the name of the baby to Zechariah. We see Zechariah reach for a writing tablet and scratch on it the definitive reply: "His name is John."

We observe Zechariah's face as he discovers that his ability to speak has returned. We take note, too, of the crowd's reaction to this phenomenon. We listen while Zechariah pours out the praise of his heart to God and, inspired by the Holy Spirit, prophesies. And we observe how the people express their awe and wonderment.

Response

We respond to this meditation by describing in our prayer journal what we have unearthed through this imaginative contemplation.

Or we put to ourselves certain questions:

Why do Christians believe in an all-powerful God—the God of the impossible?

How can our ability to believe mature and grow?

What is the value of such belief?

What was it about Mary which made it easy for her to believe?

What do I learn about faith from Zechariah and Elizabeth?

What do I learn about God's attitude to doubters as I reflect on his dealings with Zechariah?

We write the answer to some of these questions in our journal.

Or we take the phrase "Mary believed" into our day and meditate on it using the four R's described on pages 46-49.

Tell out, my soul, the greatness of the Lord,
rejoice, rejoice, my spirit, in God my saviour;
so tenderly has he looked upon his servant,
humble as she is.

For, from this day forth,
all generations will count me blessed,
so wonderfully has he dealt with me,
the Lord, the Mighty One.

His name is holy;
his mercy sure from generation
to generation
towards those
who fear him.

We listen to the words of Mary's song of praise, *The Magnificat*, on the tape; we picture Zechariah, deprived of the gift of speech because of his unbelief, and pray for those who, like him, find it hard to have faith that the promises of God will come true for them.

MEDITATION 5

Help Me to Say Yes . . .
and Help Me to Listen

Donald Coggan once wrote: "Christians believe in a God Who speaks. Ours is not a silent God, a God who sits, Sphinx-like, looking out unblinking on a world in agony." And he added, God "speaks *because he loves*. Love always seeks to communicate."

As we open ourselves to God, we shall discover the accuracy of this claim. We shall sometimes hear the still, small voice of God speaking to us, challenging us or consoling us. That in itself is moving and thrilling—yet frequently we question whether the voice we felt we heard was really God's or whether it was our own imagination working overtime. At such times we might discover something even more thrilling: that God has given an identical message to another person so that he or she can reassure us that what we have heard is indeed the voice of God.

This, at least, is what happened in Mary's experience.

Reading
We read Luke 1:39-45:

> *At that time Mary got ready and hurried to a town in the hill country of Judea, where she entered Zechariah's home and greeted Elizabeth. When Elizabeth heard Mary's greeting, the baby leaped in her womb, and Elizabeth was filled with the Holy Spirit. In a loud voice she exclaimed: "Blessed are you among women, and blessed is the child you will bear! But why am I so favored, that the mother of my Lord should come to me? As soon as the sound of your greeting reached my ears, the baby in my womb leaped for joy. Blessed is she who has believed that what the Lord has said to her will be accomplished!"*

Reflection
We imagine that we are describing these events for a person for whom this story is quite new: first, Mary's journey through the hill country, next her arrival at her cousin's home, and then the warmth and joy of Elizabeth's greeting. We use all our senses to help us to discover answers to questions like: What can I see? What do the characters look like? Who suggests to Mary that she should make this trip? What can I hear and sense and feel?

We decide to accompany Mary on the long walk, and as we travel beside her, we ask her how she feels about her secret and the privilege which is to be hers—of becoming the mother of the Messiah.

We watch Mary's reaction to Elizabeth's joyful recognition of the

Jesus, may all that is you flow into me,
May your body and blood be my food and drink.
May your passion and death be my strength and life.
Jesus, with you by my side enough has been given.
May the shelter I seek be the shadow of your cross.
Let me not run from the love which you offer,
But hold me safe from the forces of evil.
On each of my dyings shed your light and love.
Keep calling me until that day comes
When, with your saints, I may praise you for ever.
AMEN.

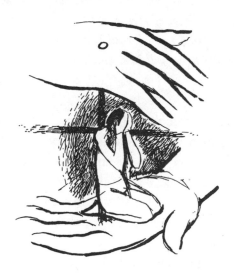

Messiah. We listen to Mary and Elizabeth as they chat; as they marvel at the miracles which have happened to each of them—the elderly lady who has conceived long after the normal childbearing age and after years of despairing of ever giving birth to a child and the teenager who has conceived at an early age without having had intercourse with a man. We listen, too, while Elizabeth tells Mary about Zechariah's vision. We watch Zechariah's attempts to join in the conversation and we ask: What do I learn from him? And from the women?

Response

We ask ourselves: Where have I been in my imagination? Have I "become" Mary or Elizabeth or have I been a bystander or, maybe, a reporter? And how have I felt about each of the people and about God?

We ask: What would I like the God of the impossible to do for me?

We linger over the memories, letting God speak to us through them. And we respond to this by writing separate prayers to the Father, the Son and the Holy Spirit.

Or we worship quietly as we listen to *The Magnificat* on the tape. We pray the prayer popularized by St. Ignatius:

Jesus, may all that is you flow into me.
May your body and blood be my food and drink
May your passion and death be my strength and life
Jesus, with you by my side enough has been given.
May the shelter I seek be the shadow of your cross
Let me not run from the love which you offer,
But hold me safe from the forces of evil.
On each of my dyings shed your light and love
Keep calling to me until that day comes
When, with your saints, I may praise you forever. Amen.

And we ask for the gift of listening prayer.

MEDITATION 6

Help Me to Say Yes . . . to What You Ask of Me

In the first five meditations we focused on some of the principal actors in the Nativity drama. Today we recap. We do this because God's mysteries never yield their full meaning at one sitting. We can return to the same story over and over again and still discover treasures we have never noticed before.

Reading
We reread Luke 1:26-38 (the Annunciation) or Matthew 1:18-25

(Joseph's dream) or Luke 1:5-25 (Zechariah's vision); we reread, too, any notes or prayers we have written in response to these passages and we pray:

Take my life and let it be
Consecrated, Lord, to Thee
Take my moments and my days
Let them flow in ceaseless praise.[1]

Reflection

We imagine that we are sitting at the window of a high-rise building in the town where we live (or a nearby town if we live in the country). In the street below, people are scurrying about their business or sauntering in the sunshine. Some are busy making an honest living. Others are hurrying to help others. Some are simply enjoying God's wonderful world. And others are scheming: planning violence of one kind or another—mugging, rape, theft, drug pushing, prostitution. Many are lonely. Some are dying of AIDS, of cancer, of heartbreak. . . . Others are content, fulfilled and thankful to God for the gift of life. Many are crying out: "Show us the way to God." "Teach us how to pray."

We imagine now that, just as God once scoured the face of the earth for people who would be willing to play a major part in his plan of redemption, so he now searches for those who will cooperate with him in rescuing our world and its people from further destruction. And this time, his eye lights not on Mary or Joseph or Zechariah or Elizabeth, but on us. We ask ourselves how it feels to be hand-picked by God; to which people do we feel most drawn? And we try to discern: What is he asking of me?

It might be something straightforward like watching the news regularly and praying for international affairs. It might be something practical like avoiding using aerosols so that we help to preserve the endangered ozone layer which protects our world. Or it might be something costly like offering to support a particular person, to relieve the suffering of a group of people or to express Christ's love and life in a specific way.

Response

We note carefully (that is, we *feel* as fully as possible) our emotional response to God's request: are we struggling, wriggling or protesting? We express these feelings to God, calling them by name, but not apologizing for them. We attempt to be real, knowing that God understands and wants to help. We allow him to speak into any resistance. And if we find ourselves able to respond willingly and generously to his request, we thank him for preparing us for this moment of grace.

When God sent his messenger to Mary, he not only invited her to be the mother of his Son but he confirmed this message to her through her cousin Elizabeth, through Joseph and through the shepherds. When he speaks to us today, he similarly confirms, through relatives, through friends and primarily through his Word that what we have heard really does come from him. So as we think back over our time of reflection, we resolve to talk to a wise friend about the fruit of this meditation, particularly if we sense God might be asking us to change the direction of our life in some major way or to offer to serve him in a particular place. As St. John reminds us, we must always test such insights against the wisdom of others.

We pray this prayer of St. Ignatius:

Lord Jesus, teach me to be generous,
to serve you as you deserve
to be served;
to give & not to count the cost;
to fight & not
to heed the wounds;
to toil & not to seek for rest;
to labour & to ask for
no reward,
save that of
knowing that
I do your holy will.

MEDITATION 7

*Help Me to Say Yes . . .
and to Be As Clay in the Hands
of the Potter*

Openness to God involves placing ourselves in his hands and begging him to reshape and remold us. Jeremiah taught us this. God once sent him to the house of a potter to watch the craftsman at work. The pot he was shaping became marred in his hands. But the potter refused to panic. He simply began again:

"So the potter formed it into another pot, shaping it as seemed best to him." (Jer 18:4)

Then God spoke reassuringly:
> *"Like clay in the hand of the potter, so are you in my hand."* (Jer 18:6)

Reading

We read Jeremiah 18:1-6 slowly and meditatively, applying to it the four R's and asking God to make us as soft, malleable clay in his hands.

> *This is the word that came to Jeremiah from the Lord: "Go down to the potter's house, and there I will give you my message." So I went down to the potter's house, and I saw him working at the wheel. But the pot he was shaping from the clay was marred in his hands; so the potter formed it into another pot, shaping it as seemed best to him.*
>
> *Then the word of the Lord came to me: "O house of Israel, can I not do with you as this potter does?" declares the Lord. "Like clay in the hand of the potter, so are you in my hand."*

Reflection

A lump of clay is full of potential. But clay, if it is to become sufficiently resilient in the potter's hands to bear the imprint of his fingerprints and become the beautiful vessel he always intended, must be malleable, free from all impurities, bubbles and grit.

When we meditate, whether we realize it or not, we are placing ourselves into the hands of the living God. And when we pray, God is at work, ridding us of the dirt which makes it impossible for him to reshape us.

We look at the picture of the lump of clay and imagine that it represents our life. We feel the hands of the potter pushing and prodding, pressing and pummelling this clay of our life.

We ask ourselves: does this feel painful or pleasant? What do I want to say to the potter?

We notice whether the fingers of God are thick, rough and chapped like some laborers' hands or long, gentle and precise like

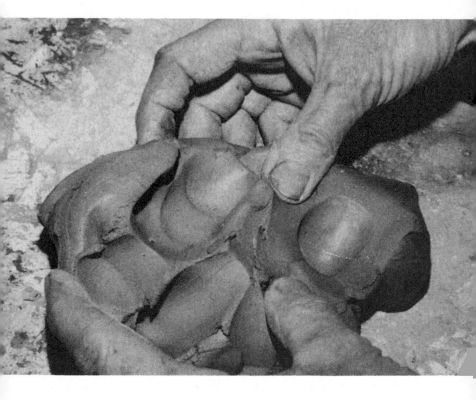

many surgeons' fingers. We notice whether the touch of God calms or distresses us and why.

Response

We write a series of prayers—one to the Father, one to the Son and one to the Holy Spirit. Or we listen to the Spirit of the living God and quietly worship God.

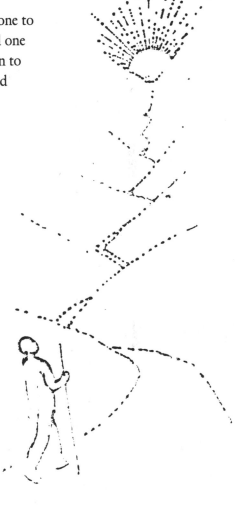

We pray this prayer:

I know
that I am called
The message was quite clear
and yet I cannot see
the how, the why.

I feel so small, so weak,
so ill-equipped
for such a task.

And yet I am prepared
to say my Yes
and undertake the risk
and enter the unknown
responding to the call.
Trustfully treading my way
the only one
that leads to life—to Him.[1]

MEDITATION **8**

Come and Worship . . .
with Mary and Joseph

Τ he Bible delights to introduce us to God's worshiping people. Worshiping people are people who know what it means to be lost in wonder, love and praise. They know to respond to their Creator; how to give him his worth-ship, how to abandon themselves to him. They know how it feels to experience the radiance and glory of the living God. Indeed, they live with a holy expectation that they will encounter him frequently. Such people were Mary and Joseph.

Reading

We read Luke 2:1-7:

> *In those days Caesar Augustus issued a decree that a census should be taken of the entire Roman world. (This was the first census that took place while Quirinius was governor of Syria.) And everyone went to his own town to register.*
>
> *So Joseph also went up from the town of Nazareth in Galilee to Judea, to Bethlehem the town of David, because he belonged to the house and line of David. He went there to register with Mary, who was pledged to be married to him and was expecting a child. While they were there, the time came for the baby to be born, and she gave birth to her firstborn, a son. She wrapped him in cloths and placed him in a manger, because there was no room for them in the inn.*

Reflection

Following a suggestion once made by St. Ignatius, we allow our imagination to roam as we pretend that Mary and Joseph have invited us to travel with them from Nazareth to Bethlehem. We have agreed to accompany them to give them any assistance we can.

As the journey begins, we picture Mary, nine months pregnant, sitting on a donkey and we remind ourselves that today a woman is not allowed to travel by plane if she is more than seven months pregnant, yet Mary is about to embark on an eighty-mile trek. We find as many ways as we can of making the journey more comfortable for her. And we observe Joseph and the creativity with which he expresses his love, concern and attentiveness to her.

We survey the scenery, drinking in the sights and sounds and smells and sensations. And we listen while Mary and Joseph reminisce. Mary recalls the day when the angel Gabriel invited her to become the mother of the Messiah. She describes, too, her visit to Elizabeth and Zechariah. Meanwhile Joseph recalls the clear way in which God showed him that he was to marry Mary and become the

Messiah's adoptive father. We marvel with them, watch their level of faith steadily rise and measure our own. We notice the reaction of this couple as we approach Bethlehem. We observe, too, the signs which suggest that Mary is about to go into labor. We watch and listen while Joseph searches for accommodations only to discover that none of the inns have vacancies. We register his relief when he is offered the shelter of the stables.

We go with Mary and Joseph into this makeshift labor room. We look around, drinking in the sights and smells and sounds as Mary goes into labor. We notice, too, our own reaction as the baby's head appears. Do we assist Joseph with the birth? Or do we want to leave Mary and Joseph to enjoy this moment of intimacy together? Do we feel useful or helpless?

Response

We ask ourselves: Where have I been? And how did I feel at various stages of the journey? We allow our feelings to surface and we tell God about them, perhaps writing about them in our prayer journal. We reflect on our relationship with Mary and Joseph and what we have learned from them recording this, too, in our journal. We ponder on that question which the Christ-child puts to us: "What do you want?" and we make our response to it.

Or we pray this prayer of St. Ignatius:

Fill us, we pray, Lord, with your light and life that we may show forth your wondrous glory. Grant that your love may so fill our lives that we may count nothing too small to do for you, nothing too much to give and nothing too hard to bear.

We play the track *Breathe on me* from the tape or we pray the Lord's Prayer.

MEDITATION 9

Come and Worship . . .
the Christ-child

C ontemplation gives rise to deep, heartfelt wonderment
and worship. To contemplate means to pay rapt and loving attention to a person or object. So to contemplate
God means to pay rapt and loving attention to him and to allow him
to do the same to us. Contemplative prayer involves being totally
absorbed—abandoned to God. Peter Dodson describes it well:
"Contemplative prayer is like taking a sun bath, like soaking up the
radiant heat of the living Christ . . . it is just being naked before God,

totally exposed to him and to his penetrating Word."

When we contemplate, our task is simply "to be silent and to let the Word of love speak to the middle of *our* being, so that it becomes heart knowledge as well as head knowledge."

If we are to do this, we may find that we need "ways in" to contemplation such as music, phrases of Scripture, pictures and quotations from books.

Reading

We ask God to ignite our hearts with the fire of his Spirit, recognizing that unless his Spirit and ours unite, true worship will evade us. We ask God, too, to rekindle in us a holy expectation that he will reveal his presence to us or speak to us in some way. And we ask for the gift of stillness in which a flicker of love for God can be fanned into a flame. Then we open ourselves to him in loving attentiveness, gaze at the picture of the newborn Christ-child and repeat over and over again the angel's proclamation (Lk 2:11):

To you is born a Savior.

Reflection

We imagine that we are kneeling beside the newborn Son of God. We gaze. We marvel. We adore. We express any emotions which surface in the ways which seem most appropriate to us: with our body, our voice, our gifts of writing or drawing. And we ask ourselves:

Is there anything I want to say to him?

Is there anything I want to do for him?

What can I learn from him?

How do I want to answer his question "What do you want?"

Is there anything he wants to say to me?

Is there anything he wants me to do for him?

We do not hurry. We relish each moment and ponder the mystery of it all.

Response

We listen to Mary's love song, *The Magnificat,* on the tape. Or we write in our prayer journal our own response of love to Love.

We sing the chorus of the well-known carol *O Come let us adore him,* or we drink in the meaning of these words:

> *O wonder of wonders that none can unfold*
> *The Ancient of Days is an Hour or two old.*[1]

Or we continue to gaze at the Christ-child, lost in wonder and adoration.

MEDITATION 10

Come and Worship . . . with the Wise Men

Williiam Temple once said of worship: "To worship is to quicken the conscience by the holiness of God, to feed the mind with the truth of God, to purge the imagination by the beauty of God, to open the heart to the love of God, to devote the will to the purpose of God."[1]

Reading

We play the song *Breathe on me* and ask God to open our hearts and minds as we meditate on his Word. We ask him, too, to give us a vigorous, adventurous faith which allows him to be God and delivers us from complacency. And we read the "history of the mystery" in Matthew 2:1-12:

> *After Jesus was born in Bethlehem in Judea, during the time of King Herod, Magi from the east came to Jerusalem and asked, "Where is the one who has been born king of the Jews? We saw his star in the east and have come to worship him."*
>
> *When King Herod heard this he was disturbed, and all Jerusalem with him. When he had called together all the people's chief priests and teachers of the law, he asked them where the Christ was to be born. "In Bethlehem in Judea," they replied, "for this is what the prophet has written:*
>
> *" 'But you, Bethlehem, in the land of Judah, are by no means least among the rulers of Judah; for out of you will come a ruler who will be the shepherd of my people Israel.' "*
>
> *Then Herod called the Magi secretly and found out from them the exact time the star had appeared. He sent them to Bethlehem and said, "Go and make a careful search for the child. As soon as you find him, report to me, so that I too may go and worship him."*
>
> *After they had heard the king, they went on their way, and the star they had seen in the east went ahead of them until it stopped over the place where the child was. When they saw the star, they were overjoyed. On coming to the house, they saw the child with his mother Mary, and they bowed down and worshipped him. Then they opened their treasures and presented him with gifts of gold and of incense and of myrrh. And having been warned in a dream not to go back to Herod, they returned to their country by another route.*

Reflection

These verses leave many questions unanswered—questions like these: Who were these "men who studied the stars"? What kind of

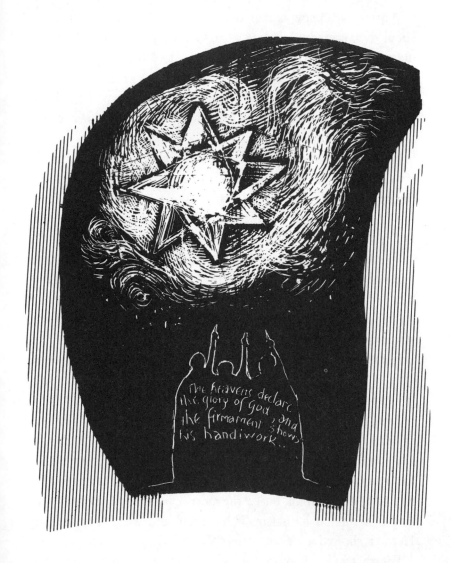

The heavens declare the glory of God, and the firmament shows his handiwork...

star was it that lured them away from family, friends and homeland? How long did the journey to Bethlehem take them? What kept them going as they traveled?

What we do know is that these men seem to have been going about their everyday business when God broke into their lives and drew them away with cords of love. Just as the shepherds were drawn to the stable at Bethlehem as though by a magnet, so these men from the other end of the social scale similarly experienced that inner, irresistible need to leave everything to follow the star which would lead them to God.

What we also know is that, down the centuries, theologians have produced a series of speculations in an attempt to answer the questions many would love to have answered.

Some, for example, claim that the men were kings from Persia. Others that they were Chaldean astrologers or philosophers. And St. Augustine insisted: "These Wise Men, what were they but the first fruits of the Gentiles? The shepherds were Israelites, the Magi Gentiles. The former close by, the latter from far away; both hasten to the Corner Stone." And St. John Chrysostom offers a fascinating suggestion about the nature of the star: "Some have thought that this star was the Holy Spirit who afterwards descended above the Lord at His baptism. . . . Some have said it was an angel." He insists that it could not have been an ordinary star for a number of reasons.

First, it moved from the east to the south ("for so Palestine lies in relation to Persia"). Second, it was visible not only by night like any other star but also "in the full light of day, which is not within the nature of any star, nor even the moon." Third, it seems to play hide and seek, peeping out at the most opportune moments: "after they had entered Jerusalem, it hid itself; and when they had left Herod it showed itself once more."

Fourth, this star appears not to have followed a course of its own. Rather, "when the Magi traveled, it traveled with them. When they halted it likewise halted, as the pillar of cloud in the desert" (Ex 13:31). And fifth, when it beamed its light over the place where Jesus lived, "it accomplished this, not by remaining on high, but by coming low, which indicates, not the action of a star, but of some rational power." He concludes that "this star was but the sign of invisible power, revealing itself in this form."

Fascinating though these suggestions are, they are, after all, only suggestions. Fantasies. But that does not prevent believers from being enriched by God while they meditate on these two verses.

We reread Matthew 2:1-12 and imagine that we have been appointed by a television company to investigate the phenomenon of the magnetic star. So we travel east, question the astrologers and their friends and neighbors and become involved in an action replay of the appearance of the star, filming as we go.

We notice what our contemplative camera captures as we survey the town or village where the "wise men" lived. We sit under the velvet night sky, film the myriad of stars which twinkle and shed their silvery light over the landscape. We focus in on that special star and notice precisely what it is that makes it different, memorable. We film the faces of the watching crowds and observe what they are doing, record their conversation and reactions, and find ourselves being caught up in the drama quite unashamedly.

As we film the preparations they make for their marathon trip, we find it necessary to explain to our viewers what inspired the Magi to saddle their camels or Arabian steeds to set off on this journey to Bethlehem. We work out carefully how we will express this. We also work hard on other aspects of our presentation: the sensations of sight, smell and sound we want to put on record to enable our viewers to become a part of this scene. Still in our role of reporter, we accompany these men on their journey, filming their companions and recording their conversations, their mealtimes, and questioning them constantly in an attempt to discover some of the reasons why they seem so convinced that, at the end of the journey, they will find a newborn king. Our filming helps viewers to detect whether these men are kind or cruel, genteel or crude.

As we travel, we observe our reaction to the Magi and their families. And we find ourselves asking whether there is anything we can learn from their courage, their dogged determination, their persistence and this inner drive which pushes them nearer and nearer to Jesus.

We observe the travelers' reaction when the star disappears and compare it with their reaction when it reappears and continues to beckon. We reflect, too, on our own reaction to God's game of hide and seek.

As we approach Jerusalem and film "the golden city," we try to capture on celluloid the ripples which spread through the caravan of travelers. We highlight their expectations as well as the sights they see.

Response

We watch an action replay of the film we have just made and notice where we have been and how we have felt as the drama unfolded.

We reflect on the sights we have seen and the sounds we have heard.

We ask ourselves what we can learn from the wise men.

We ask ourselves, too, what we can learn from the mysterious movements of God through this star.

As we recall the determination of the wise men to follow the star, we think of the countless crowds of people who search for a living faith in God and we hold them into the Father's love and mercy. We ask God to give us a heightened, holy expectancy every time we come to worship—the kind of expectancy which seems to have characterized men and women in the Old Testament and the New. They believed they would both hear God speak and encounter him. "They gathered with anticipation, knowing that Christ was present among them and would teach them and touch them with His living power."[2] And we pray:

O Lord, lift up the light of your countenance upon us
that in thy light we may see light;
the light of self-knowledge
whereby we may repent;
the light of faith
whereby to choose your will;
the light of guidance
whereby we may advance;
the light of grace
whereby we may attain;
the light of glory
which shines more and more pointing toward the perfect day
and towards you, the very Light of Light;
who lives and reigns in the brightness of
the holy and undivided Trinity
blessed for ever and ever.[3]

We listen to *To love only you* on the tape.

MEDITATION 11

Come and Worship . . .
in Bethlehem

G. od created us so that we might know, love, serve and worship him in this life and enjoy oneness with him for ever. God's purpose in creating us was to draw from us a response of love to his love outpoured. Every man, woman and child was therefore created capable of worshiping God. As the Scottish Catechism puts it: "I was created in order to worship God and to enjoy him for ever."

Reading

We read Matthew 2:1-12 (see page 134) and ask God to set us free
to worship him:

> *Lighten my eyes, O Lord*
> *that they be not blind to the wonderful things in your law;*
> *wonderful goodness*
> *wonderful love.* [1]

Reflection

We continue in our roles of television producer and reporter. And
we continue to make the epic film which aims to show viewers what
happened when the star appeared to certain Eastern astrologers.
Today we film the travelers as they leave Herod's palace in Jerusalem
and set out for the last lap of the journey—the road to Bethlehem.

We film the surrounding countryside, record the conversations
which center on the strange reaction of the insecure king, and observe the mood of the travelers and their companions. And when the
star reappears, we film it and focus on the faces of the wise men as
the familiar constellation continues to beckon them. When the star
stands still at last, we film it again before taking close-up shots of
the house over which it shines. And we show viewers the faces of
the travelers as the realization dawns that they have reached their
destination at last.

We film the wise men as they dismount and describe as accurately
as we can the mood of these men as they stoop to enter the humble
building which houses the baby King. Then we follow them.

Inside, we forget about our cameras, for there before us lies our
Creator with his mother. Our traveling companions have already
fallen on their knees in adoration.

Response

We focus our attention on Jesus and worship him in whatever way seems most appropriate. We may simply want to be present to him—fully attentive in body, mind and spirit, letting him love us and speak to us until we find ourselves responding to him honestly, spontaneously and reverently as we marvel at the mystery:

He lies in a manger, reigns in heaven, but his glory fills the heavens.

Mary is breast-feeding the King of Angels, the Savior of the world.

He who lies in this humble home holds the whole world in his hand.

Or we might echo Graham Kendrick's song *Meekness and majesty:*

Wisdom unsearchable
God the invisible
Love indestructible
in frailty appears.
Lord of infinity
Stooping so tenderly
Lifts our humanity
To the heights of His throne.
Oh, what a mystery,
Meekness and majesty,
Bow down and worship
For this is our God.[2]

Or we may want to capture in our prayer journal some of the sights we have seen, the sounds we have heard and the impressions that have come to us while we have been meditating.

We may want to record there, too, the lessons we have learned from our fellow pilgrims, from our own reactions or from Mary, Joseph or Jesus.

And we might feel inclined to write separate prayers to the Father, the Son and the Holy Spirit or to listen to *In silence my soul is waiting* on the tape.

MEDITATION 12

Come and Worship . . .
with Simeon

R ichard Foster writes:
> If the Lord is to be Lord, worship must have priority in
> our lives. The first commandment of Jesus is "Love the
Lord your God with all your heart and with all your soul and with
all your mind and with all your strength" (Mk 12:30). The divine
priority is worship first, service second. . . . One grave temptation
we all face is to run around answering calls to service without
ministering to the Lord himself.[1]

One person who seems to have learned how to resist the temptation to put service before adoration was Simeon.

Reading

We read Luke 2:22-32 and we ask God to touch us afresh with his Spirit so that we may see him in his many comings and hear his many whispers:

When the time of their purification according to the Law of Moses had been completed, Joseph and Mary took him to Jerusalem to present him to the Lord (as it is written in the Law of the Lord, "Every firstborn male is to be consecrated to the Lord"), and to offer a sacrifice in keeping with what is said in the Law of the Lord: "a pair of doves or two young pigeons."

Now there was a man in Jerusalem called Simeon, who was righteous and devout. He was waiting for the consolation of Israel, and the Holy Spirit was upon him. It had been revealed to him by the Holy Spirit that he would not die before he had seen the Lord's Christ. Moved by the Spirit, he went into the temple courts. When the parents brought in the child Jesus to do for him what the custom of the Law required, Simeon took him in his arms and praised God, saying:

"Sovereign Lord, as you have promised, you now dismiss your servant in peace. For my eyes have seen your salvation, which you have prepared in the sight of all people, a light for revelation to the Gentiles and for glory to your people Israel."

Reflection

Once again we take up our role as Mary and Joseph's helper and babysitter of Jesus. In our imagination we accompany them to the temple in Jerusalem.

As we travel from Bethlehem to Jerusalem, we look around at the scenery, listen to Mary and Joseph's conversation and the gurgles and snuffles of the six-week-old baby. We notice whether it is warm and sunny or wet and windy. And the scents and smells, the sounds and scenes along the way. In particular, we feast our gaze on the temple as it comes into view. We try to sum up in a sentence the wonder of the "golden city." And as we climb the temple steps we notice the tradesmen in the outer courts with their tables laden with doves and pigeons. We watch Joseph as he purchases his sacrifice and we enter this much-loved place of worship with the holy family.

We therefore see Simeon emerge from the wings onto the center of the stage. We notice how tall he is, how he is dressed and whether he is strong or frail. We drink in all he does and says and how we feel about him. And we reflect that, since all Jewish parents were required to present their newborn children to the priest sometime after the first month of the child's birth, Simeon must have seen countless couples come to the temple carrying their babies. Yet now, as Mary and Joseph arrive clutching their child, Simeon's heart is so open to the Holy Spirit that he discerns that this is no ordinary baby. It is the long-awaited Messiah.

Response

We recall the sight of the elderly man delighting in the young child, and we thank God for those who spend their twilight years in worship and prayer.

We ask God so to touch us with his Spirit that we, too, may be drawn closer and closer to Christ and that we may see the invisible and hear the inaudible.

We ask ourselves what we can learn from Simeon or from Mary, Joseph or Jesus. We ask, too, whether there is anything we can learn from our own reaction to these historic events. And we respond to that now-familiar question of the Christ-child: "What do you want?"

We write separate letters to the Father, the Son and the Holy Spirit telling them what is on our heart and mind and then listening and recording anything they show us or say to us.

We watch an action replay of our meditation while we write about it in our prayer journal, making a note of any fresh insights which come to us and recording any ideas and sensations which encourage or disturb us. If God seems to be asking us to change in any way, we ask for the grace to make the necessary adjustments.

We pray for all priests, pastors and people in positions of leadership, that they may be as discerning and Christ-centered as Simeon. Or we play the song *Breathe on me* from the tape.

MEDITATION 13

Come and Worship . . .
Using Simeon's Song

*S*ometimes the awareness of who God is prompts us to praise and worship him. At other times, we worship him, not simply for who he is but for what he has done for us and his wonderful world. Simeon did both and today we use his words as our "way in" to worship.

Reading

When Simeon saw Jesus, he was lost in wonder, love and praise. The song he sang to express his worship echoes down the centuries. We find it in Luke 2:29-32 and we read it aloud several times until a particular phrase or word or sentence or image draws us to itself. Then we apply to "our phrase" the four R's mentioned on pages 46-49, recognizing that this little piece of Scripture is nutritious. As St. Anselm once put it:

Taste the goodness of your Redeemer . . . chew his words as a honeycomb, suck out their flavor, which is sweeter than honey, swallow their health-giving sweetness. Chew by thinking, suck by understanding, swallow by loving and rejoicing. Rejoice in chewing, be glad in sucking, delight in swallowing.

We do that with a portion from the Song of Simeon in Luke 2:

"Sovereign Lord, as you have promised,
*   you now dismiss your servant in peace.*
For my eyes have seen your salvation,
*   which you have prepared in the sight of all people,*
a light for revelation to the Gentiles
*   and for glory to your people Israel."*

Response

We conclude this particular meditation by recording in our prayer journals "our" phrase and our response to it or by simply being present to that word of God.

We form or write a prayer which sums up what we want to say to God.

We pray:
Make me
a still place of light
a still place of love
of You
your light radiating
your love vibrating

your touch and your healing
far flung and near

to the myriads caught
in darkness, in sickness
in lostness, in fear

make a heart-centre here
Light of the world.[1]

We listen to *The Magnificat* or *Gabriel's oboe theme* on the tape, savoring the insights which have come to us.

MEDITATION 14

Come and Worship . . .
with Anna

Another person who made prayer and worship a priority
was the prophetess Anna. She was one of "the quiet of
the land"—a group of people living in Jerusalem at the
time when Jesus was born who were rather like the contemplative
monks and nuns of our own day; people who had such a burden for
God's needy world that they gave their entire lives to pray for the
coming of the Messiah.

Reading

We ask God to draw us to himself and his love as by a magnet as we read Luke 2:36-38:

> *There was also a prophetess, Anna, the daughter of Phanuel, of the tribe of Asher. She was very old; she had lived with her husband seven years after her marriage, and then was a widow until she was eighty-four. She never left the temple but worshiped night and day, fasting and praying. Coming up to them at that very moment, she gave thanks to God and spoke about the child to all who were looking forward to the redemption of Jerusalem.*

Reflection

We imagine that we are trying to describe for a small child Anna, the old lady, as she enters the temple at precisely the right time to catch sight of Simeon delighting in the presence of Jesus. We make a verbal sketch of her face and features, her height and her posture and her clothes.

We describe, too, the manner in which she approaches Mary, Joseph, Simeon and the baby and report everything she says. And we reflect on Mary and Joseph's reactions to her and her obvious joy at seeing their child. God's child.

We explain to the child we are talking to in our imagination the reason why we happen to be in the temple. We describe how we feel about being there and what we would like Jesus to do for us.

Response

We ask ourselves: Where have I been? Have I simply watched the prophetess? If so, how have I felt about her? How have I felt about the child Jesus? And how have I felt about God?

Or perhaps I have "become" Anna? If so, how did I feel?

We respond to the Christ-child's whispered "What do you want?" We record in our prayer journal the scenes we have seen, capture the sounds we have heard and the emotions we have felt.

We ask ourselves what we can learn from Anna and Mary and Joseph. We pray:

Lord Jesus, I would worship you as Anna did,
in spirit and in truth.
Like her I would
Submit all my nature to you,
that my conscience may be quickened by your holiness
my mind nourished by your truth,
my imagination purified by your beauty.
Help me to open my heart to your love
and to surrender my will to your purpose.
Like Anna
May I lift my heart to you
in selfless adoration and love. [1]

We play the chorus *Lord, you gave me everything* or listen to *Fisher of men* on the tape.

CHANGE
MY HEART
O GOD

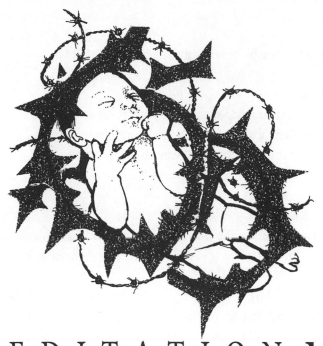

MEDITATION 15

Change My Heart, O God . . .
Until I Grow More Like Jesus

O bedience is the proof of love. Jesus proved his love with his lifelong "Yes, Father."

"Jesus was . . . obedience-in-prayer."[1] He became man because it was his Father's will. And he says of himself that to obey his Father is his "meat," his nourishment. The Holy Spirit's task is to work in us in such a way that we become more Christlike, more obedient. And just as certain skills like carpentry and cookery can be improved by watching master craftsmen at work, so we can be inspired to obey by observing the obedience of Jesus.

Reading
Obedience means self-surrender. And Jesus is just eight days old when we first observe him surrendering himself to his Father and mankind. Luke describes the event in one sentence:

On the eighth day, . . . it was time to circumcise him. (Lk 2:21)

Reflection
Once again, we assume our role as Mary and Joseph's helper and babysitter for Jesus. In this capacity we attend the child's circumcision.

We watch Mary and Joseph present the eight-day-old baby to the priest and register the reward of obedience: their joy and rightful sense of pride. We try to imagine how they might be feeling as they place God's baby into the arms of the priest and as they watch the routine operation being performed. We, too, watch the blood of the Christ-child being shed—recalling that this helpless infant is the Creator of the world. We remind ourselves of something Mary and Joseph did not know when Jesus was circumcised: that there would be another day when his blood would be poured out freely—on Calvary.

We immerse ourselves in the mystery of what is happening before our eyes without trying fully to understand it. We contemplate it by gazing on the scene, being present to it, listening to the sounds and tuning in to the atmosphere. And we turn over in our minds the implications for Jesus of this short ceremony. By submitting himself to this ritual, he was publicly identifying himself with the sinful state in which every human being is born. Yet he was sinless. Perfect. The spotless Son of God. He was also identifying fully, in racial terms, with the Jews. If he had refused to take this step, he would not have been recognized by the Jewish authorities as a son of David nor acknowledged, later in life, as a teacher in Israel. Rather, he would have been dismissed as an uncircumcised Gentile. A dog. Yet he was the Messiah, the Son of God. As an unknown writer has put it:

He was circumcised for the same reason that he was born, for the same reason that he suffered. He did nothing for himself, but all for his chosen ones. He was neither born in sin, nor circumcised from sin, nor did he die for his own sin: but it was all for our crimes . . . to be Savior is his very nature.

When the circumcision ceremony is over, we take this sinless child in our arms and turn these truths over and over in our mind. For Jesus, self-surrender and obedience required of him that he would place himself voluntarily under the Law and that he would accept the obligations required of Jewish people simply so that he might redeem them. But he goes further: he takes upon himself our impurity and guilt and undergoes the symbolic ritual of circumcision that we might be redeemed. Rescued.

Response

We recall where we have been and how we have felt. We respond to this humble, self-giving love in whatever way seems appropriate. And we drink in the astonishing fact: "He did it for me." As the child sleeps in our arms or looks into our face cooing and smiling, we hear him repeat his familiar question: "What do you want?" We tell him and wait for his reply.

We ask ourselves what we can learn from this example of humble obedience.

And we thank the little child and his Father for the love expressed in this shedding of blood we have witnessed. We remind ourselves afresh that even if we had been the only person who needed to be bought back for God by the blood of Jesus, he would have come to identify with our sin and pain. And we ask him to create within us an obedient heart.

We listen to the song *I gave my life for you* on the tape. Or we write separate prayers to the Father and the Son.

We record in our prayer journal our impressions of the circumcision ceremony—or we remain still with this example of obedience and the awareness that God is worthy of all our trust.

M E D I T A T I O N **16**

Change My Heart, O God . . .
Until I Let God Be God

Many Christians believe that God is a spoilsport and that to do the "will of God" involves pain, discomfort, disappointment and the thwarting of our own plans. If we want to go in a certain direction or if we desire a certain thing, according to this thinking, God will demand the exact opposite and spoil our fun. Obedience, therefore, seems irksome and unpleasant. It involves a yes to a course of action we shall not enjoy and the renunciation of everything we long for.

Far from endorsing these views, the Bible paints a picture of a God who loves us, beckons us, even woos us; a God who would shower us with blessings if we would give him an opportunity. This God longs that we should do this so much and knows us so well that he alone discerns what will result in our highest and ultimate good.

Reading

The name given by God to his Son pinpoints the purity of the love and the extent of the goodness of this God we worship:

He was named Jesus.

We pray the prayer of St. Ignatius: "Lord, turn my whole being to your praise and service." "Free me from being enslaved to self and motivate me, instead, to spend my entire life deepening my relationship with you and serving others for you."

Reflection

Just as we watched Jesus being circumcised, so now, still in our role as helper, we watch and listen while Joseph whispers to the priest the name "Jesus." We meditate on the word, using the method outlined in chapter two and reminding ourselves that when a Hebrew child was given a name, it was not simply a means of identification to distinguish him from other children, it was also a key to understanding his personality. His name is not so much a label as an explanation of who he is.

This is particularly true of the name Jesus. "Jesus" means "one who saves," "one who is a savior." As we gaze at the tiny child and repeat his name over and over to ourselves, we marvel that though Jesus came not only as Savior but also as King, Lawgiver, Prophet, Priest, Judge, yet it is as a *deliverer* that he desires principally to be known.

He selects a name which speaks of grace, compassion and love because overflowing, rescuing, delivering love is what he is.

As we hold this child in our arms and whisper his name, we remind ourselves of the truths we know which Mary and Joseph did not know when they gave him his name, that the Savior had, indeed, come to save his undeserving world. He had come to take upon himself our guilt and to die in our place.

It was for this purpose that he was born and grew up in Nazareth; it was to this end that he prepared during the three years of his ministry, it was this goal that he achieved when he was sentenced to death and nailed to the cross. . . . He is the Lamb of God who takes away the sins of the world. In our place he endured death and opened the way to heaven. He is the gateway to paradise.[1]

Response

We look back on the meditation and remember where we have been and what we have felt about the Christ-child and his naming.

We ask ourselves: What can I learn from Mary, Joseph and Jesus? We ask for the ability so to know God's nature that we learn to trust him implicitly and to obey him gladly.

We pray:

My Lord, who are you? Can you help me?
Can I learn to trust you?
How can I know you, how do I recognize you?
Help me to know just who you are . . .

My love is for the small things:
for the helpless; the lonely and lost; the rejected and the refugee; the frustrated and inadequate.
My love sees and embraces them all. It never rejects the worst, and always, always hopes for the best.
It is in the joy of a new day, and the despair of a lonely night.

My love is weak, broken and bruised. It feels as you often feel.
For my love is nailed to a cross, pinned on a darkened skyline.
It is a shroud in a borrowed tomb and tears on a Friday night.
Hope beyond despair, reality from the impossible; it is life after death.

My child, my love is—because I am.
And you will know me—because my love is for you.[2]

We play the Taize chant *My peace*—or we pray the Lord's Prayer.

MEDITATION 17

Change My Heart, O God . . .
Until I Know As I Am Known

G od is in love with us." That is the incredible message
which throbs through the Bible. It is so incredible that
many Christians find that there is a whole layer of their
personality which dares not accept it. And so we discover that a
discrepancy exists between the God of our mind and the God of our
"gut."

With our mind, we assent to biblical truth: that love is what God
is. But at a deeper level, at "gut level," we have concocted a God who

is more like a punitive policeman than a loving Father, a "one hundred per cent God" who accepts and loves us only when we behave well, rather than a divine lover who accepts us just as we are, or a tyrannical, killjoy God who woos us with love only to use or abuse us. This deep-down view of God, which is so far from biblical truth, sometimes stems from the picture of God we gleaned from our parents or from our Sunday-school teachers, but sometimes it proves to be a projection of ourselves:

> Invariably we create a God in our image. Because we do not love him very much, we are led to think he does not love us much. Because we do not worry much about him, we imagine that he does not worry very much about us. Because we are not very happy with him, we conclude that he is not very happy with us.[1]

When we worship such a God, we expect him to act as an avenger, an executioner or a judge to whom we must present an account of our misdeeds. Instead he sends us his Son in the form of a helpless infant to be our Savior.

Reading

Once again we meditate on the name of God's Son:

He was named Jesus.

Reflection

In the last meditation we reflected on the meaning of the name *Jesus*. We remind ourselves of the hidden meanings but recall that Jesus was given other names as well. One is Emmanuel, which simply means "God with us." Another is Christ. And another is Lord.

Christ is a Greek word which means "the Anointed One." The King. The One who came from God and through whom the royal glory of the Kingdom breaks through—

> *as when he raises the dead, heals the sick, and teaches the secrets of the kingdom of heaven. He himself rises from the dead and ascends to*

heaven. There he is now enthroned as king; God has given him all power in heaven and on earth. He holds the keys to the kingdom of death and to the kingdom of God.[2]

His lordship extends to the living and the dead. "He is the head of the church. His will must be sovereign over his people, among all who claim to be Christian. His will is to be done in heaven and on earth."[3]

Once again we imagine that we are holding God's Son in our arms at his naming ceremony. As we do so, we whisper his names over and over:

Emmanuel: God with me.
Lord Jesus Christ, Son of God
Have mercy on me, the sinner.

Response

We pray this prayer many times, perhaps listening to music like *On Eagles' Wings* while we do so.

Or we listen to the prayer *Jesus, Lamb of God* on the tape. We hear the Christ-child ask: "What do you want?" We tell him.

And we ask for the grace to know in our heart as well as our head that love was his meaning.

We repeat the various names of Jesus and ponder on the ones which strike us most forcibly.

We ask: What does this particular name mean for me at this moment in time?

We notice how we feel: peaceful or joyful, anxious or agitated or some other feeling?

We record our findings in our prayer journal and hold to God anyone known to us who cannot feel his love.

MEDITATION 18

Change My Heart, O God . . .
Until I Accept Your Love

*W*e have been taught as Christians, and presumably have believed, that "we are created for union with God"—but in
practice we seem not to dare to accept the full implications
of this on a subjective level, to really embrace it as the central truth of
our lives. Least of all, perhaps, are we prepared to trust that this is God's
passionate desire for us. (How frustrating for the Lover!)[1]

Yes. God must be frustrated when his sacrificial love meets, not a
warm response, but cold unbelief. Perhaps that is why he promises,
through the prophet Ezekiel, to remove our stone-cold hearts and
replace them with hearts that throb in response to his Word (Ezek
11:19).

When we are still and attentive to God's Word and welcoming
love, we realize that this promise has been fulfilled. Our hearts reach
out to God in love.

Reading

Even when we read a familiar passage of Scripture like John 3:16, if we apply to it the four R's and insert our own name into the text, we can be stunned into silent adoration as the truth pierces us with unexpected immediacy:

> *God so loved* _____ *that he gave his one and only Son, that* _____ *should not perish but have eternal life.*

Reflection

We apply the four R's to that verse, personalizing it by slipping our own name into it. We reflect on the nature of God's love:

> *God's love is patient,*
> *God's love is kind . . .*
> *God's love always protects, always trusts, always hopes,*
> *always perseveres.*
> *God's love never fails.* (1 Cor 13:4-8)

And we reflect on Jesus' own astonishing claim:

> *"I have loved you,* _____, *as the Father has loved me."* (Jn 15:9)

Response

We drink in this love and respond to it in whatever way seems most appropriate—by writing in our prayer journal, by gazing at the picture of the Christ-child, God's one and only Son (p. 141) or the picture of God's love outpoured at the crucifixion (p. 36), or by listening to the song *I gave my life for you* on the tape.

Or we drink in the truths through this prayer:

> *Lord my God, when Your love spilled over into creation You thought of me. I am from love, of love, for love.*
>
> *Let my heart, O God, always recognize, cherish and enjoy your goodness in all of creation.*

Direct all that is me toward your praise. Teach me reverence for every person, all things; energize me in your service.

Lord God, may nothing ever distract me from your love—neither health nor sickness, wealth nor poverty, honor nor dishonor, long life nor short life.

May I never seek nor choose to be other than You intend or wish.[2]

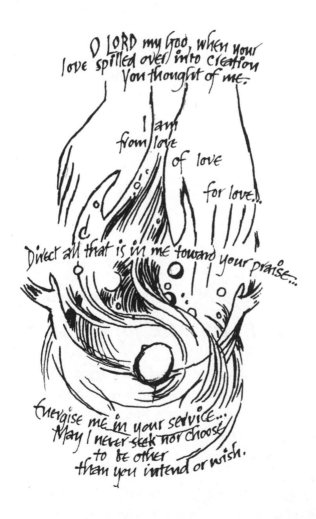

O LORD my God, when your love spilled over into creation You thought of me.

I am from love of love for love..

Direct all that is in me toward your praise...

Energise me in your service...
May I never seek nor choose
to be other
than you intend or wish.

MEDITATION **19**

Change My Heart, O God . . .
Until I Learn the Joy of Giving

M atthew describes not only the dogged determination of
the Eastern potentates who traveled to Bethlehem to
pay homage to the baby King, but the generosity which
has inspired generations of Christians.

Reading

On coming to the house, they saw the child with his mother Mary, and
they bowed down and worshiped him. Then they opened their treasures

and presented him with gifts of gold and of incense and of myrrh.
(Mt 2:11).

Reflection

True worship always results in reckless giving. One way to learn how
to love in this self-sacrificing way is to observe the generosity of
others and to receive inspiration from it.

We think back to an earlier meditation where we sat with the Holy
Trinity in the heavenly places, and we compare and contrast the
splendor with the squalor, the omnipotence with the helplessness of
the baby feeding at Mary's breast. And we remind ourselves of the
astonishing truth: "He did it for me."

We gaze from the Christ-child to the Eastern potentates present-
ing their extravagant gifts and back again, and we allow the generosity of the scene to seep into our spirit and to inspire us.

Response

We ask the Holy Spirit to create in us a similar desire to be generous; the ability and willingness to imitate the Father, the Son and
the Magi. We ask him to show us where, in times past, we have been
less than generous and to show us how he felt about our stinginess.
We beg him to change us: to show us what we can give and to
whom; to give us, too, the courage to abandon our entire selves to
him as a love offering.

We recall the faces of refugees we have seen on television or the
figures of down-and-out folk we meet near our own home or place
of work, and we reflect on the following:

We are all God's children.
I have knocked at your door
I have called to your heart
because I dream of a soft bed
because I am eager for a well lighted house.

We are all God's children.
I have knocked at your door
I have called to your heart

because I dream of a soft bed
because I am eager for a well-lighted
house.

Why do you drive me away?
Open to me, brother!

Why do you drive me away?
Open to me, brother!

　Why do you question me
About the shape of my nose
The thickness of my lips
The colour of my skin
The name of my gods?
Open to me, brother![1]

We record in our prayer journal any insights and reactions which
have featured in our meditation. And we pray:

What can I give him, poor as I am?
If I were a shepherd, I would bring a lamb;
If I were a wise man, I would do my part;
Yet what I can I give Him—give my heart.[2]

MEDITATION 20

Change My Heart, O God . . .
Until I Learn to Obey

*U*nless we are changed as a result of our worship, we need to question whether we have really been worshiping the living God. To worship means to be changed. As Richard Foster puts it: "Just as worship begins in holy expectancy it ends in holy obedience. Obedience saves worship from becoming an opiate, an escape from the pressing needs of modern life."[1]

Reading
We ask God to give round-the-clock openness to him as well as the

gift of obedience as we place the spotlight on the wise men from the East once more.

These men were like soft clay in the Master Potter's hands. They responded to God as he beckoned to them through the star. They searched diligently for him at great cost to themselves and, having eventually found Jesus, they remained in a state of day-and-night attentiveness to the divine voice. As Matthew records it:

> *God warned them in a dream not to go back to Herod; so they went back to their country by another road.* (Mt 2:12 GNB)

Reflection

We imagine that we are with Jesus and Mary and Joseph as the Magi bid them farewell. We say our own farewells to each member of the holy family, and we travel with the wise men as they start out on the homeward journey using God's diversion. We eavesdrop on their conversations, ask them how they feel about the newborn King, his parents and his living conditions—and we invite them to tell us what lasting effect this encounter with Christ has had on them.

While we travel, we focus on that quality of life which seems to be to God like a priceless treasure: "the gold of obedience." We recall the obedience of Jesus who entered our dark world to rescue us from the ravages of sin and the wiles of the Evil One. We ponder on the obedience of Mary. And we drink in what obedience has cost these visitors from the East; what it will cost Mary; and, in particular, what will be the cost to Jesus.

Response

We place our life, as though it were a lump of clay, into the hands of the heavenly Potter and ask him so to work on us that any bubbles of rebellion or disobedience may be removed slowly but gradually in order that, like each of these people in the tableau before us, we become malleable for God. And we listen, aware that God might show us a particular area of our life where he wants us to change by bringing our attitude, our will or our lifestyle into line with his.

If we feel we can, we admit to him that we are not only prepared to be worked on by him but we are ready now to go the next step: to cooperate with him.

We write about some of these mysteries in our prayer journal and ask that these well-known words may be true of us:

O worship the Lord in the beauty of holiness,
Bow down before him his glory proclaim;
With gold of obedience and incense of lowliness,
Kneel and adore him—the Lord is his name.[2]

We play the track *To love only you* from the tape.

MEDITATION 21

Change My Heart, O God . . . Until I Love As You Love

God has created me to do Him some definite service; He has committed some work to me which He has not committed to another. I have my mission. . . . I am a link in a chain, a bond of connection between persons. He has not created me for naught. . . . If I am in sickness, my sickness may serve Him; if I am in sorrow, my sorrow may serve Him. He does nothing in vain. He knows what He is about.[1]

So wrote Cardinal Newman.

Yet the sea of need which surrounds us can result in an apathy which makes of prayer an escape from the world. When God brings us face to face with such clutter, we must clear it from our path. As St. Teresa rightly reminds us: "True prayer will never happen until Martha and Mary coexist."

Reading

We read, slowly and meditatively, using the four R's, John 3:16:
God so loved the world that he gave his one and only Son.
And Jesus' exhortation from John 13:34:
Love one another as I have loved you.

Reflection

We go back, in our imagination, to the first meditation in this book where we sat with the Holy Trinity in the heavenly places and, with them, looked down on a needy world. We imagine ourselves there now, taking a cosmic view once more. We look down on the world as it turns on its axis. We gaze on the millions of starving people who struggle for survival in the "Two-Thirds World." We drink in the plight of the homeless, the destitute and the unemployed in our own country. We survey, too, the lonely rich, the bereaved, the depressed, the sick, the divorced, the dying and all who have lost hope and are aimless.

We look in turn at the Father, the Son and the Holy Spirit and sense how they feel as they watch such human suffering. And we notice our own reaction and try to register our real feelings.

Maybe we find ourselves aching inside—filled with the compassion for people which Jesus displayed when he lived among us:

When Jesus saw the crowd harassed and dejected like sheep without a shepherd, he felt with them in the center of his being (Mt 9:36). When he saw the blind, the paralyzed, and the deaf being brought to him from all directions, he trembled from within and experienced their pains in his own heart (Mt 14:14). And so it was with the two blind men who called after him (Mt 9:27), the leper who fell to his knees in front of him (Mk 1:41), and the widow of Nain who was burying her only son (Lk 7:13). They moved him, they made him feel with all his intimate sensibilities the depth of their sorrow. He became lost with the lost, hungry with the hungry, and sick with the sick. In him, all suffering was sensed with a perfect sensitivity.[2]

Or perhaps, feeling overwhelmed by the immensity of the problems confronting us, we are consumed with helplessness, powerlessness, uselessness.

We might even feel angry, guilty or inadequate.

We reread the verses above, contemplate them and let this contemplating do its own transforming work, remembering that "contemplation is about putting ourselves into the hands of God, so that he can do something with us: so that he can change and transform the way we are, the way we think, feel and behave.... Contemplation is about loving God and loving people."[3]

Response

We recall where we have been, what we have heard and seen and felt and smelled. We respond in whatever way seems appropriate: by confessing our apathy or anger in our prayer journal, by asking God where and how we might alleviate human suffering most effectively, or by resolving to spend a part of our prayer time each day in interceding for God's broken world.

We may resolve to clip a short story from a newspaper or cut a picture of a starving person from a magazine, stick it into our prayer journal and let it symbolize some of the need of the world. We gaze at the line drawing on page 182 and let it speak. Or we think of a person or people known to us who appear to be drowning in a sea of sorrow. We imagine how it might feel to become those people—or the person in the story or the picture. We put ourselves into their skin and introduce them to Christ. We wait and watch to see

what he will do and say. And we listen to see if there is anything he requires us to do for them. As we lift these situations or people to the love of God, we gather into the prayer people all over the world who suffer similarly.

Or we recall a time when we have felt rejected, lost, despised, trampled on or suffering in some way. Deliberately, we descend into the pain once more and use the experience creatively to pray for those who find themselves similarly suffering the pain of rejection, burnout, loneliness or despair.[4]

We beg God to use us in some small way, using a prayer of St. Ignatius:

O Lord Jesus Christ, take as your right, receive as my gift, all my liberty, my memory, my understanding, my will; all that I have, all that I am, all that I can be. To you, O Lord, I restore it, all is yours, dispose of it according to your will. Give me your love. Give me your grace. It is enough for me.

Or we pray *The Grail Prayer:*

Lord Jesus, I give you my hands to do your work.
I give you my feet to go your way.
I give you my eyes to see as you do.
I give you my tongue to speak your words.
I give you my mind that you may think in me.
I give you my spirit that you may pray in me.
Above all, I give you my heart
that you may love in me your Father and all mankind.
I give you my whole self that you may grow in me so that it is you,
Lord Jesus, who live and work and pray in me.

We ask God to deliver us from apathy and to help us learn the mutuality of prayer and action; to see prayer as the spring of living water which must flow out to others in a stream to save it from stagnating.

We play the song *I gave my life for you* from the tape.

CLEARING AWAY THE CLUTTER

MEDITATION 22

Clearing Away the Clutter . . .
of Sin and Guilt

*J*ust as a cluttered desk makes it almost impossible to work efficiently, so the clutter of sin and guilt obstructs our prayer life. And we need both to recognize their existence and to learn how to deal with them. One way to do this is to focus on the outrageous behavior of others and to apply biblical principles to it.

Reading
One of the most blatant examples of godlessness we have described

for us in the New Testament is the "massacre of the innocents" which Matthew records in chapter 2:16-18. As we read this horrifying story, we pray the psalmist's prayer:

Search me, O God, and know my heart; . . . See if there is any offensive way in me. (Ps 139:23-24)

When Herod realized that he had been outwitted by the Magi, he was furious, and he gave orders to kill all the boys in Bethlehem and its vicinity who were two years old and under, in accordance with the time he had learned from the Magi. (Mt 2:16)

Reflection

Herod was a tyrant-king. His cruelty was born of insecurity. Because he was insecure, if anyone threatened to topple him from the throne, he assassinated them. Before the birth of Jesus, he had already slaughtered three hundred court officials and murdered two of his sons, his wife and her mother. In Jesus he saw a new rival and, alerted by the Eastern Magi, he planned his savage attack on the babies of Bethlehem.

In our imagination, we go to Bethlehem as Herod's soldiers search for all the baby boys under the age of two. We watch while these children are butchered to death. We hear the blood-curdling cries of the children and their parents. We feel the shock which stuns the entire town. And we place the spotlight on Herod.

We feel his fear. We hear his hatred. We sense the evil holding the man in its grip. And, in our imagination, we present Herod to the risen Jesus. We listen and watch and learn while the earthly king encounters the heavenly one. We make a note of the words Jesus says, the way he looks, the gestures he makes. We observe, too, Herod's reactions to the Messiah.

Response

We recall where we have been, what we have seen and how we have reacted. We recall our own insecurities—maybe bringing to mind an occasion when we have felt particularly threatened by a person or situation. We recall our reactions, our thoughts and some of our fears and intentions. We admit to ourselves and to God that the seeds of the violence which we find so abhorrent in Herod have been germinating in us.

And we put flesh on each of our own negative emotions: the fear, the hatred, the desire for revenge. We imagine that each of these has taken the form of a person and we introduce these people to God. We watch to see what Jesus does and listen to hear what he says to us. We remind ourselves that he wants to gather us into his arms and pour peace into our pain, healing into our hurts, cleansing into our sin, and to give us the courage we need to live life his way.

We beg him to touch us in each of these ways and to show us how to change. We remind ourselves of the wickedness of Herod and the blackness of our own heart, and we use these as symbols which represent the violence which causes so much pain and destruction in our world.

We beam the love of God onto the victims of such violence— particularly those who seem unable to recover from injuries inflicted on them years and years ago. And we hold into the grace of God those who are driven by their hatred and resentment to destroy the lives of others.

We listen to *On Eagles' Wings* and ask that we may experience God's peace in the middle of all our emotional storms.

We pray:[1]

Lord Jesus our Saviour,
            let us now come to you:
Our hearts are cold;
Lord, warm them by your selfless love.
Our hearts are sinful;
    cleanse them with your precious blood.
Our hearts are weak;
    strengthen them with your joyous Spirit.
Our hearts are empty;
    fill them with your divine presence.

Lord Jesus, our hearts are yours;
    possess them always
    and only for
        yourself.

MEDITATION 23

Clearing Away the Clutter . . . of Lack of Forgiveness

I don't get mad. I just get even."

We smile when slogans like that greet us from the bumpers of people's cars. Yet such tit-for-tat thinking is part of the clutter which sometimes hinders our prayer because it is incompatible with Jesus' teaching on forgiveness.

To forgive means to let go of resentment and bitterness, hatred and anger. To forgive means to let the offending person off the hook. To forgive means to cancel the debt we feel they owe us. To forgive is therefore extremely costly. And it happens in stages.

Forgiveness begins by feeling the full brunt of the pain and recognizing that we have every reason to feel hurt as well as every right to want to retaliate: to hit back; to hurt as we have been hurt. But forgiveness continues by making a deliberate choice to refuse to exercise that right. By engaging the will, forgiveness drops any accusations we might wish to make and switches off the gas which has kept our anger simmering.

Forgiveness even goes further. While refusing to deny that we have been hurt, it searches for acceptable and significant ways of serving the one who harmed us in the first place. This, at least, is forgiveness following the pattern of Jesus.

Reading

We read Matthew 2:16-18 and focus in particular on the way the prophecy of Jeremiah (Jer 31:15) is being fulfilled:

> *When Herod realized that he had been outwitted by the Magi, he was furious, and he gave orders to kill all the boys in Bethlehem and its vicinity who were two years old and under, in accordance with the time he had learned from the Magi.*
>
> *Then what was said through the prophet Jeremiah was fulfilled:*
> *"A voice is heard in Ramah,*
> *weeping and great mourning,*
> *Rachel weeping for her children*
> *and refusing to be comforted,*
> *because they are no more."*

Reflection

We picture the little town of Bethlehem no longer basking in the reflected glory of its newborn King but steeped, instead, in shock, sorrow and grief. In particular, we observe the bereaved women weeping, mourning and refusing to be comforted. We attempt to identify with them by putting ourselves in their shoes, imagining how it might feel to have one's baby boy brutally murdered by a madman. We imagine how, had it happened to us, we might feel about Herod. And how we might feel about God.

We step into our own shoes and recall a time when we have been hurt or offended by someone, either deliberately or unwittingly. We recall the pain or the grief, the anguish or the bewilderment which paralyzed us at the time. We watch an action replay of the circumstances. And we visualize the people who inflicted the wounds.

We bring Jesus into the scene and introduce him to each of the people concerned. We express to the individuals and to Jesus the hurt or the anger or the bewilderment which still gnaws away inside us refusing to be silenced. We watch and listen while Jesus interacts with these people who have battered us. We do not force ourselves to forgive if we are not ready, but we do keep at the back of our mind that phrase from the Lord's Prayer: "Forgive us our sins *as we forgive those who sin against us.*" "Forgive . . . as we forgive." We ask ourselves whether we are ready to let go of our ambivalence or wrath.

When we have been hurt in the way the women in Bethlehem were, or even when we have been crushed or rejected in less drastic circumstances, forgiveness does not come easily, quickly or naturally. By God's grace it can come gradually. We can therefore afford to wait and to be patient with ourselves. If we are not yet ready, we express to God our inability to forgive, recognizing that he accepts us even though we come clutching the clutter of hard feelings, venom and sourness. If we find we are ready to forgive, it sometimes helps to act out this letting go.

Response

We look at the picture of Christ's cross or, if we have a cross in our prayer place, we kneel or sit there and in our hands we hold a real or imaginary stone. This stone represents our smoldering rage, irritation or grudges. We hold this stone symbol in our clenched fist, come with it to the foot of the cross and, when we feel ready, uncurl our fingers and place it at Jesus' feet. We pray the prayer Jesus prayed from the cross: "Father, forgive them, for they do not know what they are doing" (Lk 23:34).

When our hands are empty, we cup them as a sign that we are ready to receive God's love for the person who has bruised our spirit and his cleansing from the sin which has soiled our own life.

Or we kneel or sit in front of the cross of Christ and pray several times *The Jesus Prayer:* "Lord Jesus Christ, Son of God, have mercy on me a sinner." As we inhale, we breathe in the life and love of Jesus. As we breathe out, we let go of the poisonous feelings we have been harboring.

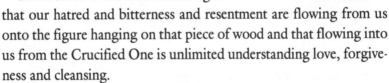

Or we come to the cross and imagine that our hatred and bitterness and resentment are flowing from us onto the figure hanging on that piece of wood and that flowing into us from the Crucified One is unlimited understanding love, forgiveness and cleansing.

We might need to confess that we are not yet ready to let go, in which case we imagine that our hatred or grudge is enfleshed. It becomes a person whom we introduce to Jesus. We watch and listen while he talks to this part of us which he both accepts and wants to change.

Or we allow Jesus to draw us to himself, to hold us, to love us with our hurt and our hatred, so to pour his compassion into us that, in time, he draws forgiveness from us.

We listen to *The Lord's Prayer,* taking seriously the phrase "Forgive us . . . as we forgive."

We play from the tape the prayer *Jesus, Lamb of God.*

MEDITATION 24

Clearing Away the Clutter . . .
of Unbelief

*L*avish, protective, unconditional love is what God is. He has our best interests at heart. As Mother Julian of Norwich put it, "love was his meaning":

Would you know your Lord's meaning in this? Learn it well. Love was his meaning. Who showed it you? Love. What did he show you? Love. Why did he show you? For love. . . . And so I saw full sure that before ever God made us, he loved us. And this love was never quenched nor ever shall be.

But God moves so mysteriously in our lives that we do not always feel enfolded by love. When disappointments deal their body blow or when crises crush us, we may be sorely tempted to doubt the love of God or to imagine that his love extends to everyone except us. In this meditation, we focus on the way God tested Joseph and Mary's trust and how he demonstrated to them the truth of Isaiah 55:8-9:

> *"My thoughts are not your thoughts, neither are your ways my ways," declares the LORD. "As the heavens are higher than the earth, so are my ways higher than your ways and my thoughts than your thoughts."*

Reading

We read Matthew 2:13-14, 19-23:

> *When they had gone, an angel of the Lord appeared to Joseph in a dream. "Get up," he said, "take the child and his mother and escape to Egypt. Stay there until I tell you, for Herod is going to search for the child to kill him."*
>
> *So he got up, took the child and his mother during the night and left for Egypt. . . .*
>
> *After Herod died, an angel of the Lord appeared in a dream to Joseph in Egypt and said, "Get up, take the child and his mother and go to the land of Israel, for those who were trying to take the child's life are dead."*
>
> *So he got up, took the child and his mother and went to the land of Israel. But when he heard that Archelaus was reigning in Judea in place of his father Herod, he was afraid to go there. Having been warned in a dream, he withdrew to the district of Galilee, and he went and lived in a town called Nazareth. So was fulfilled what was said through the prophets: "He will be called a Nazarene."*

Reflection

We picture Mary and Joseph in their tiny home in Bethlehem and, in our imagination, we become their helper, Jesus' babysitter.

We recall the excitement and euphoria which surrounded the visit of the wise men. To remind us of that visit, we finger their extravagant gifts: the gold, the incense and the myrrh. And we cherish the child—the center of their worship.

We notice what the house is like, where it is situated, how it is furnished. We observe the family routine. We watch the child grow, endearing himself to family and friends alike.

In the middle of one night, we receive the startling command from God: "Escape to Egypt." Hastily, we push a few personal belongings into a bundle, wrap the infant Son of God in a coarsely woven blanket and steal out into the night as swiftly and silently as we can.

We carry the Christ-child in our arms. We watch Mary and Joseph carefully as we discern their feelings, and we become aware of our own emotions as we glance at the shadows and shapes of sleeping Bethlehem. In the moonlight, we look at our small charge smiling up at us and remind ourselves of John's claim: "God so loved the world that he gave his one and only Son." God's Son. We recall the urgency of God's warning and the news that Herod had placed a death sentence on Jesus. We talk with Mary and Joseph about the protective love of God and discover the secret of their calm trust.

We watch the sun, like a red ball, roll over the horizon. We drink in the freshness and newness of the day, hear the music of the dawn chorus—but recall the reason for the journey and register our emotions. Watching for possible pursuers, we press on and on toward Egypt, carrying in our arms that tangible reminder of God's love: his only Son.

In Egypt, we watch while Mary and Joseph find a new home. We settle there with them, observing what the new home looks like and feels like, how it is furnished and what the new rhythm of life consists of. As news of the massacre of Bethlehem's babies filters through, with Mary and Joseph, we marvel that God worked in such a mysterious way to protect the Savior of the world.

Response

We watch an action replay of the nightmare flight into Egypt and ask ourselves:

Where have I been? And how have I felt?

What can I learn from Mary?

What can I learn from Joseph?

And what can I learn about God?

We hear the Christ-child whisper: "What do you want?" and we make our response—perhaps in writing in our prayer journal or perhaps verbally or by simply soaking in his love.

Aware that we have been holding in our arms the Sustainer of the world, we pray:

Turn my whole being to your praise and service.

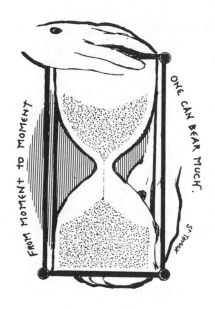

FROM MOMENT TO MOMENT

ONE CAN BEAR MUCH.

S. TORREY

MEDITATION 25

Clearing Away the Clutter . . .
of Frustration

G od's clocks keep perfect time." That was a favorite saying of Corrie ten Boom—even while she was a Dutch prisoner of war.

But for those of us who jet around the world carrying our leatherbound "organizers," our pocket year-planners, our five-year diaries or our portable computers and cellular phones, a clock which moves one tick at a time seems frustratingly slow. We easily forget the supreme value of the present moment, "the now," or, as an obscure seventeenth-century mystic, Pierre de Caussade, preferred to call it, "the sacrament of the present moment."[1] And such forgetfulness and frustration hinder our prayer.

Reading

We reread Matthew 2:19-23:

> *After Herod died, an angel of the Lord appeared in a dream to Joseph in Egypt and said, "Get up, take the child and his mother and go to the land of Israel, for those who were trying to take the child's life are dead."*
>
> *So he got up, took the child and his mother and went to the land of Israel. But when he heard that Archelaus was reigning in Judea in place of his father Herod, he was afraid to go there. Having been warned in a dream, he withdrew to the district of Galilee, and he went and lived in a town called Nazareth. So was fulfilled what was said through the prophets: "He will be called a Nazarene."*

Reflection

We imagine that we are living with Joseph and Mary and Jesus in their refugee home in Egypt and that we have had the privilege of watching God's Son grow from a baby into a toddler. But one morning, Joseph announces that once more God has spoken to him in a dream. "We are to go back to Israel."

We help Joseph and Mary pack their few belongings, respond to the child's questions and saddle the well-traveled donkey.

As we set out on our journey, we look at the now familiar scenery and drink in the beauty of the sights and sounds and smells for the last time—savoring each second and entertaining the inquisitive child by pointing out the palm trees, the camels and the well-loved people.

As we travel, too, we describe for Jesus the cave where he was born, the shepherds who came to visit him on the night of his birth and the little house from which he was taken to the temple when he was greeted by Simeon and Anna. We look forward to showing him these scenes of his birth.

But as we come closer to Bethlehem, we discover that, though the dreaded Herod has died, his ruthless son, Archelaus, has succeeded him to the throne. Perplexed, we wait for further instructions from God. They come in the form of another dream. In response to that dream, we bypass Bethlehem and head, instead, for Nazareth.

As we retrace our steps to this familiar little town, we tell the toddler at our side about the visit to his mother of the angel Gabriel, we describe the dreams God gave to his father and we explain how mysteriously God gave his aunt Elizabeth the gift of a child, John. And as we talk, we see that, so far, one tick at a time has been quite fast enough.

We climb the steep hill from Cana of Galilee to Nazareth, notice the changes which have been made and drink in, too, all that is familiar. We go with Joseph and Jesus to that little cave which used to be Joseph's carpenter shop. We hear the joyful, welcoming greetings of family and friends. And we settle, with Mary, Joseph and Jesus, into the family home, and ponder on the mystery which is God.

Response

We think back over the mysteries we have been contemplating, reflect on where we have been and ask ourselves what we can learn from Mary and Joseph, from Jesus and from the step-by-step guidance God gave.

In the light of what we have read and seen and felt and heard, we reflect on Pierre de Caussade's claim "God makes of *all* things sacraments of love," and his question "Why should not every moment of our lives be a sort of communion with the divine love?"[2]

We beg God to train us to receive from him all the experiences of life (both joyful and painful) with the awe and gratitude with which we receive the bread and wine at Holy Communion.

We ask too, for the grace to live "one tick at a time," trying, as Pierre de Caussade reminds us, not to let apprehension about the future or regret about the past flood into the present to make us miserable.[3]

We listen to the track *In silence my soul is waiting* on the tape and ponder on a well-loved saying of St. Teresa: "From moment to moment one can bear much."

Or we meditate on the following prayer, using the method of meditation outlined in chapter two: Reading, Receiving, Responding, Resting.

I was regretting the past
and fearing the future.
Suddenly my Lord was speaking:
"My name is I AM." He paused.
I waited. He continued.
"When you live in the past,
with its mistakes and regrets,
it is hard. I am not there.
My name is not I Was.
When you live in the future,
with its problems and fears,
it is hard. I am not there.
My name is not I Will Be.
When you live in this moment,
it is not hard. I am here.
My name is I AM."[4]

MEDITATION 26

Clearing Away the Clutter . . .
of Self-Hatred

*S*ometimes the person we refuse to forgive is ourselves. We recognize the truth: that we are attracted by sin, biased to sin, encrusted by sin, lured up spiritual cul-de-sacs by temptation and filled with self-loathing. We know in our heads that forgiveness is what Jesus came to give us. We even reach out to receive his love. Yet we cannot take the final step and forgive ourselves and this obstructs our prayer.

Reading

We read John 1:21 and Matthew 3:13-17:

> *They asked him, "Then who are you? Are you Elijah?"*
>
> *He said, "I am not."*
>
> *"Are you the Prophet?"*
>
> *He answered, "No.". . .*
>
> *Then Jesus came from Galilee to the Jordan to be baptized by John. But John tried to deter him, saying, "I need to be baptized by you, and do you come to me?"*
>
> *Jesus replied, "Let it be so now; it is proper for us to do this to fulfill all righteousness." Then John consented.*
>
> *As soon as Jesus was baptized, he went up out of the water. At that moment heaven was opened, and he saw the Spirit of God descending like a dove and lighting on him. And a voice from heaven said, "This is my Son, whom I love; with him I am well pleased."*

Reflection

We imagine once again that we have been invited to take up our cameras and make a documentary of the life of Jesus. Today, we visit Nazareth just as Jesus explains to Mary that the time has come for him to leave this tiny town to begin his public ministry. We film him as he bids his mother farewell. And we walk with him from his home to the Jordan where John the Baptist has already begun to prepare people for his coming.

As we walk and while we capture on camera the vineyards and orange groves, the farmers sowing their seed and the undulating hills, Jesus unfolds his plan of salvation—first placing it in its historical context.

He recalls how excited he and his Father and the Spirit were when planet earth was created. He points to the scarlet poppies, the anemones and the wild orchids and describes the delight with which they studded the fields with such flowers. He points to the fading stars and moon and to the sun gliding up over the horizon and describes the delight with which they designed these symbols of their magnificence and mystery. And he recalls with what joy they created men and women to relish to the full these good gifts.

We film the shadow which crosses his face when he remembers how Satan so skillfully and subtly persuaded God's people to believe, not that God is good, but rather that he is a spoilsport, intent on depriving them of fulfillment and life—and when he relates how the people he had made turned from him to pursue personal pleasure, prestige and power.

But true love never gives up, he says to the camera. For this reason, when his Father discerned that the time was ripe, he volunteered to leave the spaciousness and splendor of heaven to rescue planet earth and its people from inevitable destruction. Even the name his Father chose for him, "Jesus," sums up the nature of his mission. "Jesus" means "savior." And, among other things, a savior is one who brings "wholeness" and "the freedom to develop without hindrance." We take a close-up shot of his face again as he hints at the price which must be paid if the world is to be rescued from the collision course which threatens its existence.

While we drink in these mysteries and attempt to find a way of translating them for our viewers, we catch our first glimpse of John the Baptist. We focus the lens on him and on the crowds of people who throng around him. We film, too, the green waters of the River Jordan.

We watch John the Baptist's face as he spots Jesus, his cousin, and film the two men as they greet one another. And we listen to Jesus' insistence that he should identify with the sin of the world by descending into the waters of baptism.

We stand on the banks of the river, camera in hand, as John wades into the water with "the Lamb of God who takes away the sin of the world." As we watch the fast-flowing waters engulf the figure of Jesus, we recognize that he is identifying with our sin and we ask ourselves how it might feel for the sinless Son of God to be coated with the sin of the entire world. We reflect on the relationship which we developed with him while he was a child and which deepened on the walk to the Jordan. We reflect, too, on the plan of salvation he spelled out to us. And we hear him inviting us to place on his submerged body the sin and the failure which have been defeating us and clinging to us so tenaciously.

Response

We rerun the film we have just made and savor Paul's summary of the Savior's mission: "He became sin for us." We concentrate on our own reaction—our desire or our reluctance to let go of our guilt and failure.

As we watch the video and see Jesus descend into the water, we might want to pray *The Jesus Prayer:* "Lord Jesus Christ, Son of God, have mercy on me a sinner," and imagine our sin—past, present and future—floating down the Jordan. Or we might need to confess that, though we see the scapegoat Lamb of God with the eyes of our imagination, we are not yet ready to let go of our self-loathing. We respond, instead, to Jesus' question: "What do you want?"

Or we might simply want to be present to the mystery we have witnessed, the Son of God plumbing the depths of our darkness and sinfulness, and marvel: "O happy fault which gained for us so great a Redeemer."[1]

We play the tracks *Jesus, Lamb of God* and *I gave my life for you* on the tape. Or we pray:

Anoint the wounds
of my spirit
with the balm
of forgiveness
pour the oil

of your calm
on the waters
of my heart
take the squeal
of frustration
from the wheels
of my passion
that the power
of your tenderness
may smooth
the way I love
that the tedium
of giving in
the risk of surrender
and the reaching
out naked
to a world
that must wound
may be kindled
fresh daily
to a blaze
of compassion
that the grain
may fall gladly
to burst in the ground
—and the harvest abound. [2]

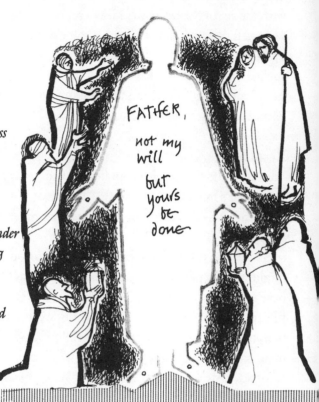

FATHER,
not my
will
but
yours
be
done

MEDITATION 27

Clearing Away the Clutter . . .
of Self-Centeredness

F rom our emergence from our mother's womb into this world, our almost immediate experiences of conscious reality proceed to confirm the illusion that we are the centre of the universe: the crying infant is comforted; hungry, it is fed. Its every need is attended to for its very survival and growth; everything is given, nothing demanded of it. . . . 'Watch out for No. 1!' becomes an implicit and instinctive motto. . . .

This basic egocentrism is opposed to God-and-other-centredness. . . .

This is why conversion may be described as a 'shifting of one's center',
away from narcissistic self-love and self-serving, to the self-giving love
and serving of God and others. [1]

One of the simplest ways of visualizing this self-orientation is to
write the word SIN in capital letters on a sheet of paper or in a
prayer journal; to focus on the letter I, draw a circle around it and
let the symbolism speak for itself. When we do this, we have drawn,
in diagrammatic form, the essence of sin. For sin is placing ourselves
at the center of our world so that it is self we serve rather than God.

Reading

We read Philippians 2:5-8, applying to it the four R's and slipping
our own name into the text:

Your attitude, _____, should be the same as that of Christ Jesus:
Who, being in very nature God,
did not consider equality with God something to be grasped,
but made himself nothing,
taking the very nature of a servant,
being made in human likeness.
And being found in appearance as a man,
he humbled himself
and became obedient to death—even death on a cross!

Reflection .

We return, in our imagination, to the place where we began in the
first meditation: in heaven with the members of the Holy Trinity.
We hear their dismay as they watch our wonderful world, their
creation, hurtling to disaster.

We take particular notice of the second person of the Trinity, the
Son of God, and observe the splendor which surrounds him and the
privileges which he enjoys. We feel the intensity of his love for the
world and the people who inhabit it, his love for us personally. And

we watch while he lays aside his majesty, strips himself of splendor, tears himself from his Father's presence, empties himself of the glory and clothes himself, instead, with the frailty of human flesh. We gaze at the picture of the crucifixion and remind ourselves of his degradation and humiliation.

Response

We reread the verses from Philippians and compare ourselves with Christ. We ask:

Does my life revolve around Christ and his kingdom or around me?

Have I been pulled by the desire for power, prestige, popularity or anything else from making Christ number one?

If so, what am I going to do about it?

What can I learn from the example of Jesus?

We pray the prayer of St. Ignatius as we recognize that our need to be changed is constant: "Lord, turn my whole being to your praise and service."

We spell out our feelings about ourselves and our lifestyle in our prayer journal. Or we marvel at the height and depth and breadth and length of God's love.

We return to that word SIN which we wrote at the beginning. We look carefully at the I with the circle around it, draw a line through the I so that it forms a cross and thank God that, through Christ, he has made it possible for us to embody the claim St. Paul once made: "Now it is no longer I who live, but Christ who lives in me" (Gal 2:20).

We look again at that word SIN and recognize that, with the circle around the I, it has been changed into SON. Symbolically, we blot out the I completely and ask that God would continue to work in us so that the God-shaped gap inside us might indeed be filled by the Son instead of by self. But we recall the words of a hymn which reminds us that this turning away from self-centeredness to God-centeredness is the work of a lifetime:

O let me feel Thee near me:
The world is ever near;
I see the sights that dazzle,
The tempting sounds I hear;
My foes are ever near me,
Around me and within;
But Jesus, draw Thou nearer,
And shield my soul from sin.

O let me hear Thee speaking
In accents clear and still,
Above the storms of passion,
The murmurs of self-will;
O speak to reassure me,
To hasten or control;
O speak and make me listen,
Thou Guardian of my soul. [2]

We beg the Potter to go on reshaping, remolding and refining us—through prayer and through circumstances—until we have become the shape and size he always intended us to be.

We play the chorus *Spirit of the living God* on the tape.

MEDITATION 28

Clearing Away the Clutter . . . Today—and Every Day

*T*o pray is to change. To pray means to abandon ourselves to the skillful hands of the Potter; so to yield to him that he is able to make of the lump of our life the lovely expression of his creativity he always intended we should be.

Reading
We read meditatively, using the four R's, 2 Timothy 3:16-17 and Hebrews 4:12:

All Scripture is God-breathed and is useful for teaching, rebuking, correcting and training in righteousness, so that the man of God may be thoroughly equipped for every good work. . . .

For the word of God is living and active. Sharper than any double-edged sword, it penetrates even to dividing soul and spirit, joints and marrow; it judges the thoughts and attitudes of the heart.

Reflection

We remind ourselves that God's revealed Word, the Bible, is one of the sharp tools the Potter uses to chip away superfluous parts of us; that this book is unique. As one author puts it:

In one sense, we have a book like any other book. It has words, ideas, grammar, figures of speech, history, poetry. . . . In another sense, however, the Bible is completely different from any other book. The Bible is God's inspired Word and when we read it, we are not examining it; it interprets us. As God's Word it has a life of its own and we must *listen* to what God says to us through it.[1]

God's Word not only contains a life of its own, it is charged with a unique, life-changing dynamism which possesses the power to challenge and change our lives. That, at least, was what J.B. Phillips found when he paraphrased the New Testament. "It seemed to speak to my condition in a most uncanny way," he wrote.

This is what we, too, will find—particularly if we embark on the slow, contemplative reading which has been recommended in this book.

The contemplative experience is that the Word of God has a fine cutting edge, sharp and fine as a scalpel. It is the cutting edge of truth, spoken in love. The Word has the power to get right under the skin—to probe our innermost thoughts and desires. It is a kind of gentle open-heart surgery. There is no anesthetic; only the love of God and his patient ability to probe the heart. . . . The contemplative way of prayer allows God to use the sword of the Spirit.[2]

Response

We gaze at the picture of the almost-completed vessel in the Potter's hands. We ask ourselves a series of questions:

What is God saying through this picture?

What is he saying *to me* at this moment in time?

Supposing I could become the pot, how might I feel?

Supposing I was the potter, how might I be feeling?

We ask God to go on and on transforming us. We use a prayer like this:

Unstop my ears that they fail not to hear
the ceaseless music of your mercy
the harmonies of your truth
your own still, small voice.
Penetrate my mind, that all the day long
it may search out the deep things of your Spirit,
in your light see light,
and be centered on you.

We play the song *Breathe on me* on the tape.

Notes

Chapter 1

[1] Richard Foster, *Celebration of Discipline* (Hodder and Stoughton, 1980), p. 90.

[2] Maria Boulding, *The Coming of God* (SPCK, 1982), pp. 7-8, 1.

[3] From a card produced by West Malling Abbey. Line drawing by Sr. Theresa Margaret.

[4] M. Basil Pennington, *Centering Prayer* (Image Books, 1982), p. 22.

[5] Andre Louf, *Teach Us to Pray* (Darton Longman and Todd, 1974), p. 22.

[6] George Appleton, ed., *The Oxford Book of Prayer* (Oxford University Press, 1985), pp. 56-57.

[7] My adaptation of the prayer "Before Meditation" from Dean Eric Milner-White, *My God My Glory* (SPCK, 1967), p. 8. © The Friends of York Minster, 1954, 1967, reproduced by permission of the publisher.

[8] Pennington, *Centering Prayer*, p. 21.

[9] Brother Ramon, *A Hidden Fire* (Marshall Pickering, 1985), p. 68.

[10] Michel Quoist, *Prayers of Life* (Gill and Macmillan, 1963), pp. 77-78. Used by permission of the publishers.

[11] Alfred Monnin, *Life of the Cure d'Ars* (Burns and Lambert, 1862), p. 55.

[12] Guy Brinkworth, *Thirsting for God* (Mullan Press, 1970), pp. 7-8.

[13] George Sinker, *Jesus Loved Martha* (St. Hugh's Press, 1949), p. 11.

[14] Ibid., p. 12.

[15] Ibid., p. 14.

[16] Brother Kenneth and Sister Geraldine, *Pray With* . . . (CIO, London, 1971), p. 11.

[17] Foster, *Celebration of Discipline*, p. 13.

[18] John Greenleaf Whittier (1807-1892), "Dear Lord and Father of Mankind."

Chapter 2

[1] Catherine de Hueck Doherty, *Poustinia* (Fountain, 1975), p. 20.

[2] Brother Ramon, *A Hidden Fire*, p. 68.

[3] Words from a card produced by West Malling Abbey. Line drawing by Sr. Theresa Margaret.

[4] Foster, *Celebration of Discipline*, p. 24.

[5] Victor Poucel, *The Body at Prayer* (SPCK, 1978), p. 7.

[6] Morton Kelsey, *The Other Side of Silence* (SPCK, 1977), p. 112.

[7] Pennington, *Centering Prayer*, p. 202.

[8] Thelma Hall, *Too Deep for Words: Rediscovering Lectio Divina* (Paulist Press, 1988), p. 1.

[9] Pennington, *Centering Prayer*, pp. 31-32.

[10]Gerard W. Hughes, *God of Surprises* (Darton Longman and Todd, 1985), p. 47.
[11]Eleanor Farjeon (1881-1965), "Morning Has Broken." Used by permission.
[12]Frances Ridley Havergal (1836-1879), "Take My Life and Let It Be."
[13]Hall, *Too Deep for Words*, p. 43.
[14]Ibid., p. 19.

Chapter 3
[1]Martin Luther, quoted in Donald Coggan, *The Sacrament of the Word* (Fount, 1987), p. 23.
[2]Coggan, *The Sacrament of the Word*, pp. 168-69.
[3]*The New Bible Dictionary*, Norman Hillyer, ed. (IVP, 1982).
[4]Peter Toon, *Meditating Upon God's Word* (Darton Longman and Todd, 1988), p. 38.
[5]John Powell, *He Touched Me* (Argus, 1974), pp. 78-79.
[6]Hughes, *God of Surprises*, p. 78.
[7]Kelsey, *The Other Side of Silence*, p. 234.
[8]Toon, *Meditating Upon God's Word*, p. 95.
[9]Ibid.
[10]Foster, *Celebration of Discipline*, p. 22.
[11]Hughes, *God of Surprises*, p. 31.
[12]Margaret Hebblethwaite, *Finding God in All Things* (Fount, 1987), p. 69.
[13]Hughes, *God of Surprises*, p. 37.
[14]H.R. Bramley (1833-1917).
[15]Hebblethwaite, *Finding God in All Things*, p. 76.
[16]Ibid., p. 133.
[17]Hughes, *God of Surprises*, pp. 96, 99.

Chapter 4
[1]Brother Ramon, *A Guidebook to the Spiritual Life*, Peter Toon, ed. (Marshall Pickering, 1988), p. 122.
[2]Ibid.
[3]Evelyn Underhill, *Light of Christ* (Longman, Green and Co., 1944), p. 27.
[4]Ibid., p. 28.
[5]Margaret Holliday. *What Is a Retreat?* (Methodist Retreat Group, 1983), pp. 9-10.
[6]J. Veltri, *Orientations* (Loyola Press, 1979), p. 7.
[7]Inspired by Gerard W. Hughes in a talk in Westminster Abbey, February 1989.
[8]Foster, *Celebration of Discipline*, p. 177.
[9]Underhill, *Light of Christ*, p. 102.

Meditation 1
[1]*The Daily Missal* (Collins Liturgical Publications, 1975), p. 55.
[2]Caryll Houselander in *The Mary Book*, F. J. Sheed, ed. (Sheed and Ward, 1950), p. 49.

[3]Ibid., p. 48.
[4]My adaptation of a meditation found in the Exercises of St. Ignatius.

Meditation 3
[1]George Appleton, *One Man's Prayers* (SPCK, 1977), p. 4. © George Appleton 1967, 1977. Reproduced by permission of the publisher.

Meditation 4
[1]J. B. Phillips, *Your God Is Too Small* (Wyvern Books, 1960), pp. 123-24.

Meditation 6
[1]Frances Ridley Havergal, "Take My Life and Let It Be."

Meditation 7
[1]Henry Rohr, *Set Me Free* (Spectrum Publications, 1972).

Meditation 9
[1]H. R. Bramley (1833-1917).

Meditation 10
[1]William Temple, quoted in Foster, *Celebration of Discipline,* p. 138.
[2]Ibid., p. 141.
[3]Milner-White, *The Light of Grace,* quoted in *My God My Glory* (SPCK, 1954), p. 158.

Meditation 11
[1]Source unknown.
[2]Graham Kendrick, © 1986 Make Way Music. Administered by Thankyou Music. Used by permission.

Meditation 12
[1]Foster, *Celebration of Discipline,* p. 140.

Meditation 13
[1]Card produced by West Malling Abbey.

Meditation 14
[1]Joyce Huggett, *Approaching Christmas* (Lion, 1987), p. 86.

Meditation 15
[1]Louf, *Teach Us to Pray,* p. 28.

Meditation 16
[1]Per-Olof Sjorgen, *The Jesus Prayer* (Triangle, 1986), p. 24.

[2]Dave Hopwood, *Acting on Impulse* (Lee Abbey, 1987), p. 28.

Meditation 17
[1]Hughes, *God of Surprises.*
[2]Sjorgen, *The Jesus Prayer,* p. 24.
[3]Ibid.

Meditation 18
[1]Hall, *Too Deep for Words.*
[2]Jacqueline Syrup Bergan and S. Marie Schwan, *Love: A Guide for Prayer* from the Take and Receive series (St. Mary's Press, 1985), p. 11. Used by permission of the publisher. All rights reserved.

Meditation 19
[1]Rene Philombwo, a Cameroon writer quoted by J. Veltri in *Orientation.*
[2]Christina Rossetti (1830-1894), "In the bleak midwinter."

Meditation 20
[1]Foster, *Celebration of Discipline.*
[2]J. S. B. Monsell (1811-1875), "O Worship the Lord in the beauty of holiness."

Meditation 21
[1]Produced on a small card.
[2]Henri Nouwen, *Compassion* (Darton Longman and Todd, 1982), p. 17.
[3]Peter Dodson, *Contemplating the Word* (SPCK, 1987), pp. 4, 18.
[4]Inspired by a talk given by Charles Elliot in Westminster Abbey, January 1989.

Meditation 22
[1]The prayer which follows was written by St. Augustine of Hippo.

Meditation 25
[1]Pierre de Caussade, *Self-abandonment to Divine Providence* (Fontana, 1933), p. 65.
[2]Ibid.
[3]Ibid.
[4]Helen Mallicoat, quoted on an Argus poster.

Meditation 26
[1]The Service of Light for Holy Saturday, *The Sunday Missal* (Collins Liturgical Publications, 1975), p. 211.
[2]Dom Ralph Wright, quoted by Boulding, *The Coming of God,* p. 122.

Meditation 27
[1]Hall, *Too Deep for Words,* p. 19.

[2]J. E. Bode (1816-1874), "O Jesus, I have promised."

Meditation 28
[1]Phillips, *Your God Is Too Small,* pp. 123-24.
[2]Dodson, *Contemplating the Word,* pp. 4, 18.